Shape, Design, T

ADVANCED LABANOTATION

VOLUME I

PART 2

Shape, Design, Trace Patterns

by

Ann Hutchinson Guest

and

Rob van Haarst

Dance Books • Alton

First published in 1991

This edition published in 2011 by
Dance Books Ltd., Alton, Hampshire, UK

ISBN 978-185273146-5

For examples taken from scores to illustrate particular points we gratefully acknowledge permission granted by the following:

Paul Taylor, James Cunningham, Louise Chan Wong Shuk Chun, William Gibbons (for Tamiris' choreography), Anna Jooss Markard and the late Leonide Massine.

All Labanotation graphics in this book were produced electronically using the Labanotation editing software CALABAN (Computer-Aided Labanotation), created by Andy Adamson at the University of Birmingham. For information on this product write to

Andy Adamson
Department of Drama and Theatre Arts
P.O. Box 363
Birmingham, B15 2TT England.

Contents

Introduction to the Series

The initial idea for this series was to write "Part 2" of the book *Labanotation - The System of Analyzing and Recording Movement* (Hutchinson 1977).[1] It would be a manual for Labanotation along the same lines as the first book, but dealing with more advanced and specialized aspects of the Labanotation system, such as Gymnastics, Partnering, Floorwork and Acrobatics, Swimming, Movements of the Hands, Fingers and Face, Use of Props.

When we started working on this book, it soon became clear that the task was an enormous one. To bring out all the material as one textbook would be impractical because it would take years to complete all the chapters.

Instead, chapters are being published individually, making the material more readily available. Subjects which seemed more immediately needed, such as supporting on other body parts than the feet, design drawing, etc. have been given priority.

Labanotation and *Kinetography Laban*, *Motif Writing* and *Structured Description*

The subject of this book is *Labanotation*, the name given in the United States to the system of movement notation originated by Rudolf Laban in Germany and first published in 1928. Most European notators and dance scholars refer to the system as *Kinetography Laban*. There are some small differences in notation usages, and occasionally in symbols and rules, between Labanotation and Kinetography. Since 1959 the International Council of Kinetography Laban (ICKL) has been a successful platform for unification between practitioners. Differences are now minor so that mutual understanding of scores is ensured. Kinetography rules and usages are catalogued in Albrecht Knust's *Dictionary of Kinetography Laban (Labanotation)* (1979).

The aim of the present text is to provide a guide to the *Structured Description* of movement, the fully-fledged notation offering a determinate description of the movement progression by detailing choreographed (or otherwise set) actions. A different and complementary approach is *Motif Description (Motif Writing)*, the use of symbols to represent movement ideas and concepts, providing a general statement concerning the theme or motivation of a movement. We show in this text how Design Drawing, a powerful tool in Motif Description, can be incorporated in Structured notation scores.

Source materials

Information on advanced Labanotation usages has not been generally available. Much use is made by practitioners of the comprehensive theoretical account of the system in Knust's 1979 Dictionary already mentioned. The textbook *Dance Notation: Kinetography Laban* by Maria Szentpál, published in Hungarian between 1969 and 1975 is not readily accessible to readers outside Hungary. The *Advanced Labanotation* series offers new research on the Labanotation system and is completely up-to-date.

Advanced Labanotation contains systematic discussion of other usages and, where needed, comments on the history of symbols and rules and the reason they are included in the Labanotation system. The material presented is based on the two textbooks already mentioned, as well as on earlier writings of Knust and Szentpál. Another major source of information are the proceedings of 15 ICKL Conferences. Reference materials also include personal discussions and correspondence with specialists such as Sigurd Leeder and Valerie Preston-Dunlop as well as with members of the Dance Notation Bureau in New York.

In many cases, writing an advanced text of this kind has meant breaking new ground: the intricacies of writing kneeling, sitting and lying for instance are not covered in the 1979 Knust Dictionary. Some recent developments in the system such as "DBP" (Directions in relation to the location of Body Parts) and "Design Drawing" (the subject matter of the present volume) came too late to be included in any other major text.

Research involved

A major concern in the research for this book has been the screening of one rule against another to check applicability in all contexts. Often this has led to discoveries producing new arguments for or against a certain way of writing.

Labanotation is rapidly developing and becoming accepted as a tool both in research and in education. Each of these fields has specific requirements: there is a call for maximum flexibility of the notation system, so that it can provide general and simple statements for particular purposes and at the same time be very precise for specific application. In dance research, precision has increased to the point where we are forced to consider questions about the system that only ten years ago did not seem important, let alone when the fundamentals of the system were devised. In this new text we have tried to take these different needs into account while respecting the system as it has been handed down to us and is now used by people all over the world.

Multi-purpose book

This is a multi-purpose text. It is designed as a textbook-style explanation for students of Labanotation at different levels: the more detailed information is presented in smaller print and can be skipped by elementary or intermediate students.

The Index is elaborate so that the text can be used as a dictionary. The Notes contain systematic annotations disclosing the research that underlies the main text, and are intended for those who use Labanotation for academic purposes or to investigate the system itself. They also identify the origin of examples taken from choreography.

Also available

Canon Forms shows how to write in Labanotation the choreographic device of Canon often used in stage choreography. It analyses different forms of canon and shows how they have been applied in choreography by Balanchine, Taylor and in movement choirs in Germany in the 30s. This material gives insight in canon structures and also shows how complex movement for more than one performer is handled and laid out on the paper.

Forthcoming issues

Kneeling, Sitting, Lying is a comprehensive manual for the writing of movement when the body is not supported on the feet. Not only does it analyse in great detail how one can get up from lying, lie down from standing, roll from sitting onto the knees, etc., and how these movements are notated, but it also offers a complete survey of Labanotation rules about distance, timing, systems of reference, weight distribution and floor contact that apply to Labanotation as a whole and underlie any writing of 'floorwork'.

Floorwork and Acrobatics completes the theory on movements on the floor (standing on hands and feet, supporting on the hands...) and offers many reading examples taken from choreography that include 'floorwork' and basic acrobatics. It also gives a full account of revolutions of the body and their recording in Labanotation.

Centre of Weight explores the possibilities of recording in Labanotation movements in which placement of body weight is of particular importance:

falling, leaning, balancing and weight shifting. It includes many examples from modern dance technique.

Future publications will include chapters on Relationship, Movements of Hands, Fingers and Face, and Dynamics.

Preface

Movement may have as its aim the forming of a shape, a static design made by the whole body or a part of the body, or the activity may be centered on the tracing of a design in the air, usually described by an extremity, in particular the hand or fingers. Shapes and designs may even be formed by more than one person or by entire groups.

Shapes and trace designs (trace patterns) may literally evoke an imaginary object, as when a mime artist makes a roof over his head using gestures and shapes of arms and hands; they may be used symbolically, as in the 'V for Victory' finger sign, or purely decoratively, as many straight and circular forms in choreography.

Whether used in Motif Description or in detailed notation, indicating the desired design or shape gives the performer an immediate idea of how to approach the resulting position (when a shape is to be made) or the resulting movement (when a design is to be drawn in the air). For use in Motif Description the reader is referred to *Your Move* by Ann Hutchinson (1983: pp. 173-174). The present text deals with the explicit indication of shape and design as part of detailed Labanotation scores.

Choreographed movement often clearly presents a shape or design aspect. Sometimes this aspect is not notated as such but remains implicit in indications not directly referring to shape. For instance, group formations are usually recorded in Labanotation by means of floor plans of the stage rather than in terms of shape writing. However, in many cases the design drawing and shape writing symbols discussed in this book provide a useful shorthand as well as a quick indication of the movement essentials.

Section 1 introduces the basic symbol for 'shape' present in all design and shape indications. Trace designs in the air are examined in part I (sections 2-27) and indication of static shape in part II (sections 28-32). Part III (sections 33-37) shows how design drawing is used in full notation context.

Acknowledgements

"Design Drawing" was acknowledged as a feature of the notation system by the International Council of Kinetography Laban (ICKL) in 1975. It has been further refined thanks to ICKL discussions in subsequent years (see note 2 on page 84 for details).

Comments on previous drafts of this book from many colleagues have been extremely helpful in compiling the present version. We are particularly grateful to Sheila Marion and Lucy Venable for their extensive proofreading efforts and judicious remarks.

Special thanks are also due to Andy Adamson, Lecturer in Dance at the University of Birmingham. As part of his ongoing research into computer-aided publishing of Labanotation Mr. Adamson helped and advised us with the production of the notation graphics in this book using CALABAN (Computer-Aided Labanotation). We are grateful for his advice on programming and production matters and for his hospitality.

For repeated proofreading and work on all previous versions of this book we are much indebted to Jane Whitear Dulieu and her eagle's eye. Intermediate versions of the Labanotation in this book were drawn and checked by Nancy Harlock whose ability with autography has been an important contribution to this work.

Shape, Design, Trace Patterns [2]

1 Sign for Shape

1.1. The 'diamond' symbol, **1a,** is used in Labanotation to indicate spatial aspects. It is modified by the addition of a single horizontal line to indicate 'shape', as in **1b.**

1.2. The sign for 'a shape' is used as a pre-sign before a pictorial representation of the desired shape. Used in this way it indicates a body pose or posture of a particular configuration. For this application, see Part II, p. 55.

I. DESIGN DRAWING

2 Design Path

2.1. Many gestures, particularly in mime, trace recognizable designs or patterns in the air. Since these tracings are essentially paths, the method of writing them is based on the idea of a path. The sign for 'a shape' shown in **1b** is modified into a path sign. Ex. **2a** illustrates various path signs; **2b** is the sign for a design path.

2.2. In the following explanations, for brevity and because of established practice, the terms *design* and *trace pattern* will be used interchangeably to refer to the pattern traced.

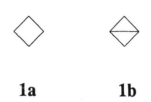

1a   **1b**

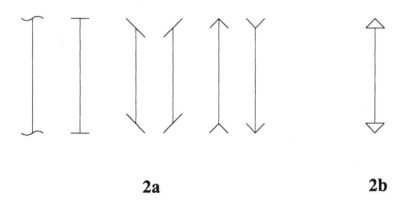

2a   **2b**

3 Representation of the Design

3.1. Exs. **3a-d** are typical examples of designs. The desired design is placed within the path sign, **3e-g**. The black dot in each example indicates where the pattern commences.

3.2. These designs are thought of as two-dimensional unless otherwise indicated. Three-dimensional designs are more rare.

> For three-dimensional shape, see 28.3 (**28n-p**); cf. shape of surface, section 19, change of surface in design drawing, section 23.

3.3. A typical action involving designs is to 'write' in the air an imaginary design; usually, the hand or fingers trace the design but the whole arm is involved in the movement. Such actions may be written as design paths rather than through standard directional indications. Standard descriptions may not only be complex, but also do not focus attention on the movement idea, namely tracing a path.

4 Indication of Timing

4.1. As with other path signs, the length of the design path indicates the timing, the duration of the action. Ex. **4a** is of short duration; it takes 3 counts. Ex. **4b** takes twice the time of **4a**, while **4c** takes all of nine counts.

> 4.2. As with all path signs, the timing starts at the base of the sign and extends to the end. If the triangles are to be excluded from the timing, a double horizontal line device is used (a similar device also serves to exclude body part pre-signs from timing, cf. **6i**). In **4d** timing starts only *after* the triangle at the base of the sign, and likewise concludes before the top of the sign. Compare this with the standard sign of **4e** which relates to the same time span. Dotted lines are added here for comparison only.
>
> Exs. **4f-i** (see next page) use the device of **4d**.
>
> Timing of pre-signs, 6.4. Exact timing, section 34.

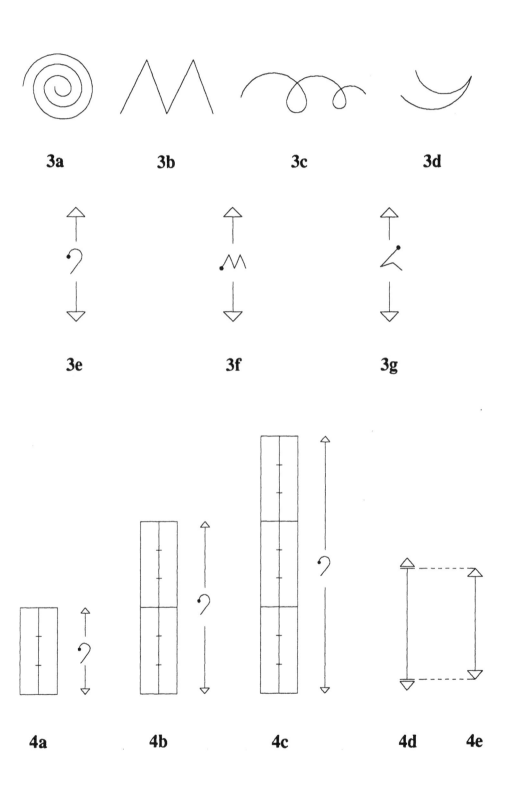

3a   3b   3c   3d

3e   3f   3g

4a   4b   4c   4d   4e

4.3. **Variations in speed.** If motion along the design is not at an even speed, the design may be divided into segments and indication given of the time taken for each segment.

4.4. In **4f**, small strokes drawn across the line of the design indicate individual sections. The vertical line of the path sign (the time line) is marked off into sections corresponding to the timing for each of the segments of the design. In **4f**, the staff has been included on the left, showing the design to extend over three measures of 3/4 and one count of the fourth measure. The first part of the design occurs on count 1. The next segment takes two counts. The third segment takes all of the second and third measures, while the last segment takes one count.

4.5. **Auxiliary time lines.** Ex. **4g** shows how this timing can alternatively be indicated by action strokes placed alongside the path sign in an addition bracket. For other examples, see **34b, 37b'** (with accent sign).

4.6. If indication of duration as in **4g** is placed too far away from the staff, the immediate visual relationship with the musical beats is lost. To avoid this, the addition bracket can act as an auxiliary time line indicating beats and measures; action strokes indicating the timing of each segment are then easily interpreted, **4h**.

4.7. Ex. **4i** shows the design broken into pieces, each piece placed within the correct time section of the path sign. This particular notation relates more directly to the timing on the staff, but the visual impact of the overall design is lost. Some designs can be handled this way more easily than others; the writer must find the clearest, most logical way.

4.8. **Time signs.** Signs for 'accelerando' and 'ritardando' can be placed next to the design path in an addition bracket to indicate speeding up or slowing down in performing the trace path within the given time. Ex. **4j** indicates starting slowly and then speeding up; **4k** indicates starting quickly and slowing down.[3]

4.9. Two different relative speeds in a given length of time can be indicated for one design by placing a stroke across the line of the design where the change in speed occurs. In **4l**, the curved part of the design is to be performed more quickly (shorter duration), the straight part more slowly (longer duration).[4] Such indication of timing is relative, of course. For precise counts for each section, the design must be segmented and the counts for each segment shown, as in **4f-i**.

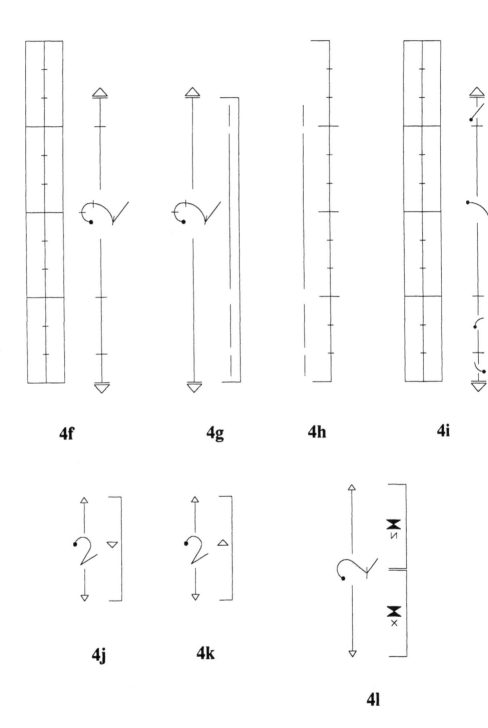

4f   4g   4h   4i

4j   4k

4l

5 Indication of Segments in the Design

5.1. Should there be any doubt as to the sequence for segments of a pattern, small numbers placed next to each segment remove all question. In **5a**, from number 1 through 4 a figure-eight pattern results.

5.2. In **5b** there is no crossing as in a true figure-eight. As this may not clearly be seen from the actual drawing of the design, the added numbers make the pattern clear.

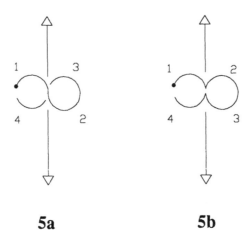

5a   **5b**

6 Parts of the Body Performing the Design

6.1. **Analysis.** A design in the air may be made by:

(1)   a limb or the extremity of a limb segment - finger (fingertip), knee, elbow, foot, etc.
(2)   another body part (head, chest, pelvis, etc.)
(3)   a body surface (palm, sole of foot, surface of lower arm, etc.)

Type (1) designs for limb *segments*, for instance for the upper or lower arm, can be viewed as being traced by the extremity of that segment, i.e. the upper arm moves as a result of an elbow design and the lower arm as a result of a wrist design.[5]

6.2. Achieving a design traced by an extremity of the body usually requires involvement of neighboring parts. Note the following facts concerning designs produced by parts of the body:

> When the **whole arm** moves we are usually aware of the design being drawn by the extremity (the hand).
> See examples **33a-c, 33l-n, 33o, 33u, 36c**, section 37 (handling props).

> Designs produced by the **hand** alone are limited to what can be achieved through wrist flexion and lower arm rotation, possibly combined with some changes in how the hand itself is held.
> See examples **33g-h, 33t, 34a, 36b**.

> In trace patterns for the **wrist**, the lower arm moves in space; the upper arm may assist in the action; the hand is unimportant and may be held out of the way so that attention is on the path of the wrist. See examples **33e-f, 33q, 33s**.

> When the **elbow** traces a design, the upper arm moves in space and the lower arm is passively kept out of the way.

> Mobility in the shoulder joint makes many small **shoulder** designs possible, usually imagined as occurring on a side surface.
> For surfaces, see section 11, cf. section 17. Examples, **33h-h'**, **35a**.

> A design created by a **finger** will be small, unless involvement of the hand or perhaps more of the arm is stated. Cf. 7.1 (7a), 7k-m, **36b**.

> A pantomimic gesture in which the **palm** or the back of the hand is the part creating the design might be an action such as polishing a window (a vertical gesture) or polishing a table (a horizontal gesture) (cf. section 11). The palm will face the surface on which the design is being 'drawn'. Involvement of the whole arm is usually required. See examples **33d, 33s, 35d**.

> Flexibility in the waist allows the **chest** (rib cage) to create 'designs'; these often involve shifting actions. See example **35b**.

Circular designs made by the **pelvis** are not uncommon. Flexibility in the waist and in the hip joints as well as passive reactions in the legs and ankles make pelvic designs possible. See examples **35c-d.**

The **legs** and **parts of the legs** follow the same general rules as the arms and their parts in relation to trace patterns. See examples **33i-k, 34a.**

Designs may be 'drawn' by the top of the **head,** or the **nose.** Such designs are achieved by flexion and rotation in the neck. In designs for the **eyes** the eyeballs move with or without accompanying head movement (**35e**).

A special case is the design path for the **center of gravity** (center of weight), see 35.6 (**35f**).

Details on degree of involvement of neighboring parts, section 7.

6.3. **Way of writing.** To indicate the body part doing the tracing, the design path is written in the appropriate column on the staff or the appropriate body part sign is placed as a pre-sign before the design path.

In **6a** placing the design path in the appropriate column shows the whole leg performing the trace design. Ex. **6b** shows a design for the right arm. In **6c** this is stated out of context through use of the pre-sign for the right arm. Exs. **6d-g** use pre-signs to show, respectively, the pelvis, the left index finger, the head, and the palm of the right hand performing designs.

Various ways of combining design path signs and other indications, see 9.1-.

6.4. Pre-signs placed before the design path are included in timing. When they are to be excluded from timing, short double horizontal lines can be used:

ex. **6h**: the pre-sign for the hand is included in the timing and the design begins on count 1 of the first measure;

ex. **6i**: the presign is excluded from timing. The movement begins on count 3;

ex. **6j**: the pre-sign is excluded from timing because it falls below the double bar line of the staff.

6.5. Because of timing or spacing, it may be necessary to bow the pre-sign to the design path as in **6k**; however, this is not a preferred usage.

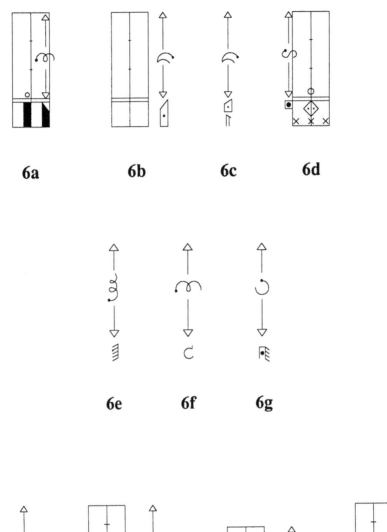

6a   6b   6c   6d

6e   6f   6g

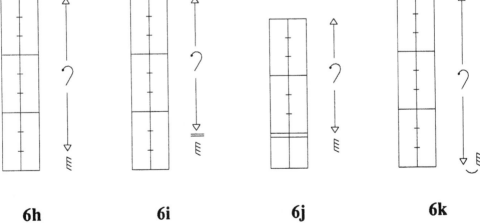

6h   6i   6j   6k

7 Degree of Involvement of Neighboring Parts

7.1. Depending upon placement of the limb and situation of the design, it may be necessary explicitly to indicate inclusion of neighboring parts. For example, 'writing on the wall' may use a finger as if it were a pen, but then it is likely that the hand, the lower arm, or even the whole arm will be involved.

> For introduction to manner of performance of design paths for various body parts, see 6.2.

7.2. A design traced by the right index finger can be achieved by just moving the finger itself (i.e. using only the joint between the phalange and the metacarpal bone), or by involving the wrist, elbow and shoulder joints to varying degrees. In **7a** the movement takes place mainly in the metacarpo-phalangeal joint; as a neighboring part, the hand may be slightly involved. If the design described by the top of the finger is mainly caused by articulation in the shoulder joint, the design must be written for the right arm as a whole, not for the index finger. Any degree of articulation or lack of articulation in the various joints can be stated if this is important.

> On the understood performance of design tracing, see also section 14.

7.3. Involvement of body parts in design tracing may be:
(1) an unintentional passive reaction to the main movement
(2) a definite accompaniment to it
(3) an intentional exclusion of a neighboring part.

7.4. **Passive reaction.** In **7b** the hand reacts passively to the finger movement. In **7c** the lower arm is affected, and in **7d** the whole arm is affected, i.e. takes part passively.

7.5. **Active involvement.** In contrast to the passive participation of exs. **7b-d**, the following examples state active participation. In each of them the finger is the focal point, but other parts of the arm actively participate.

7e: the hand accompanies the finger (the hand is included);
7f: the lower arm is included;
7g: the whole arm is included;
7h: the lower arm is explicitly included while the upper arm reacts passively.

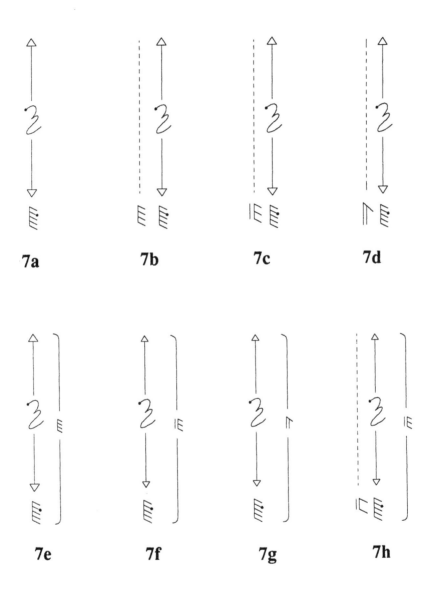

7a   7b   7c   7d

7e   7f   7g   7h

7.6. Exclusion. We can indicate specific exclusion by using an exclusion bow (**7i**). The part to be excluded is placed inside the small curve.

7.7. In **7j** the lower arm is specifically excluded from a hand design; the movement as described uses only wrist flexion. This exclusion can also be described as holding the lower arm still, as in **7k** where a space hold for the lower arm is indicated.
See also example **33k**.

7.8. Body part leading. Ex. **7l** shows an arm design performed with outstretched index finger. The impression will be of the index finger tracing, but the movement is one of the whole arm. (This can also be written as in **7g**).
In **7m** the index finger *leads* the arm in tracing the design. The result is a complex movement that cannot be performed too quickly and clearly involves wrist flexion. Exact performance of this movement depends on context but the general idea is clear. [6]

8 Size of the Design

8.1. In general, a design made by a finger will be smaller than one drawn by the hand, a hand design will be smaller than one drawn by the lower arm, and so on. The size of the design may be left open, or it may be indicated in general terms by stating the scale, the amount of space used, as in **8a-f**. Note the signs for 'as small as possible' (**8e**) and 'as large as possible' (**8f**). [7]

8.2. These signs can be placed adjacent to the design path in an addition bracket, as in **8g**, or within the design path itself, as in **8h**.
For examples, see **33m**, **33u**, **35d**.

8.3. Some designs cover more space than others; specific details of limb direction, the distance the limb travels, the area in which the design takes place, etc. can all be indicated when specific performance is needed.

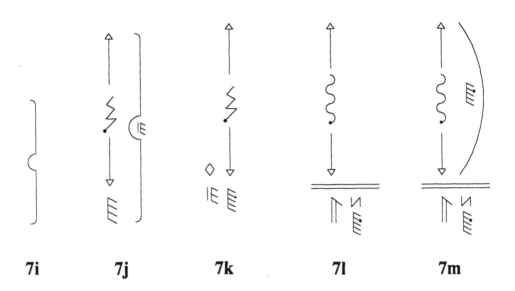

7i   **7j**   **7k**   **7l**   **7m**

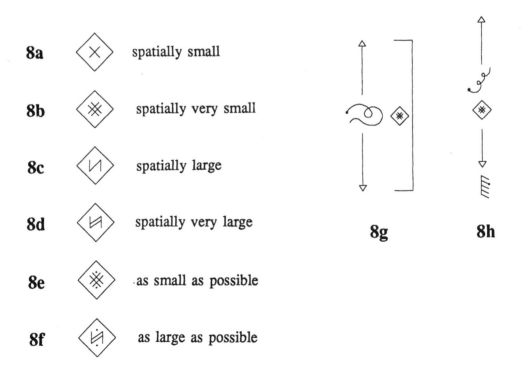

8a   spatially small

8b   spatially very small

8c   spatially large

8d   spatially very large

8e   as small as possible

8f   as large as possible

8g   **8h**

9 Placement of the Design

9.1. **Design paths in context.** In this section we will consider the combination of design paths with other instructions in the context of detailed movement notation. Design path signs can be used on their own or in conjunction with other notation indications, notably direction symbols for the tracing body part.

9.2. In **9a** the design path sign is placed in the arm column as part of a sequence of arm movements. Direction symbols indicate movements of the arm before and after the design. Part of the arm sequence is signified by the design path on its own.[8]

For other examples, see **33a, 33l-m, 33u,** cf. **33i.**

9.3. In **9b** the arm movement is one of tracing a design; the general area in which the design is to take place is stated. See 9.7 (**9e-k**) for details.

9.4. In **9c** an arm movement is described in the conventional way using a sequence of direction symbols, but this sequence is more specifically described by an added design path sign. The design path expresses the appropriate movement idea and will determine more closely the shape of the path and the exact manner of performance.

For other examples, see **33b-c, 37c-d.**

9.5. In **9d** direction signs indicate a simple displacement of the arm to the right; the added design path indicates a circling pattern traced by the arm while it moves to the right, thus superimposing movement on what is described by the direction sign. The desired movement is a combination of the two instructions.

For displacement during design drawing, see also section 22.

9.6. In exs. **9a-d** the movement has been kept simple for clarity; to identify the movement, design drawing is not strictly necessary. Depending on the need the notator will choose to describe the movement by design paths, direction signs (and/or other indications such as deviation pins), or both, in any of the ways discussed above. Design paths alone, with or without indication of size of the design, are often suitable for Motif Writing and general descriptions. In detailed notation, specification of some kind is usually desirable, particularly in relation to the situation of the design.

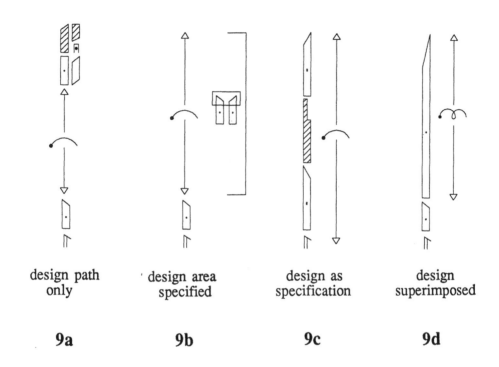

design path   design area   design as   design
   only   specified   specification   superimposed

   9a   **9b**   **9c**   **9d**

9.7. **Situation of the design in space.** The general placement in space of the body part performing the design can be indicated by combining the sign for *an area* with the appropriate direction symbol. Ex. **9e** shows the general area of /left forward low diagonal; **9f** shows the general area of right forward high diagonal.[9] Ex. **9g** shows the left arm making a zig-zag design starting in the general area left forward low.

9.8. If the design is to remain in the stated general area (i.e. to be centered in it), this is specifically indicated by placing the required area sign within a bracket outside the design path. In **9h** the right arm makes an outward spiraling pattern in the general area of right forward high.
   For reading example, see **34b**. Cf. section 15 on starting point of design.

9.9. If the pattern progresses from one general area into another, we use the appropriate area signs to indicate the starting and destination areas. Ex. **9i** shows a 'squiggle', a wavy line beginning in the area left forward diagonal low finishing in the area left forward diagonal high.

9.10. The starting and finishing areas can also be indicated as in **9j**. Here the destination is stated at the end by linking the signs with a bow. Cf. **9n**.
   The pattern of **9k** occurs in the general area in front of the body from the left to the right diagonal.
   See reading example **37e**.

9.11. Specific placement at the start for the limb performing the pattern can be indicated in the usual way by a direction symbol. In **9l** the left arm starts forward low; in **9m** the right arm starts side high.

9.12. A direction symbol may be vertically bowed to the end of the design path to indicate specifically where the limb is to finish, as in **9n**.

9.13. Note that the situation of a design can be more explicitly stated by giving the 'surface' upon which it is 'drawn'. The analysis and indication of surfaces for designs are discussed in sections 11-12.

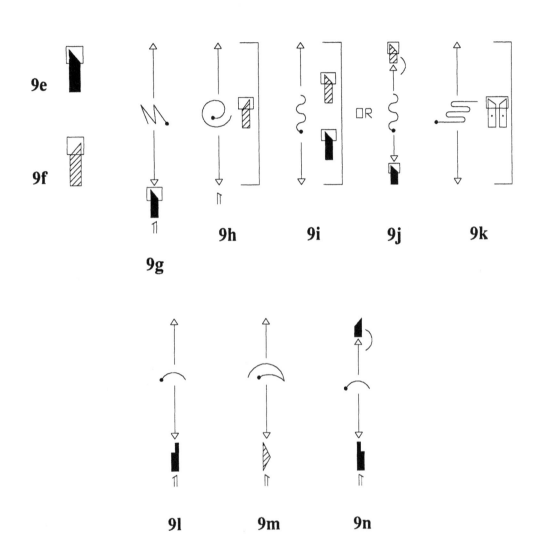

10 Repetition of a Design

10.1. Repetition of an identical pattern is best indicated with repeat signs. This can be handled in the following ways:

(1) repetition of the design path, **10a**.
(2) repetition of the pattern within the path, **10b**.
(3) use of a number to indicate the number of times the pattern is to be performed, **10c** or **10c'**.

In each of these examples the same design is traced three times.
 In (2) and (3) the movements are understood to be evenly spaced in the time allowed. In (3) the number used to indicate the repetition must not appear to be part of the design; the notation of **10c'** may therefore be clearer than **10c** in some instances.
For other examples, see **33a, 33e, 33k, 33l, 33s, 35a**, cf. **35e-e'**.

10.2. When the limb is displaced while performing a closed design the shape of the overall design changes. In **10d** the repeated design of a complete circle is to be performed while the limb moves to another direction. This pattern is usually better written as in **10e**.
See also design and whole body displacement, 22.4 (**22d-g**).

10.3. **Unemphasized return to starting point.** The design to be repeated may be a closed design, like a figure-eight which ends where it started, or an open design like the number 7. To repeat an open design for which there is no change of limb location, a swift, unemphasized transition comparable to a preparation or upbeat must take place. On paper this transition can be shown by a dotted line. Ex. **10f** shows two closed designs; in contrast, the examples of **10g** are open designs with dotted lines indicating an unemphasized return to the starting point.
See also example **35a**.

10.4. Exs. **10h** and **10i** illustrate repetitions of a design for which there is no change in direction for the limb; the design occurs each time in the same place. The time needed to go back to the starting point of the design, i.e. the movement represented by the dotted line, is included in the time for the design path.
See also **35a** and, for moving to the starting point of the design, section 15.

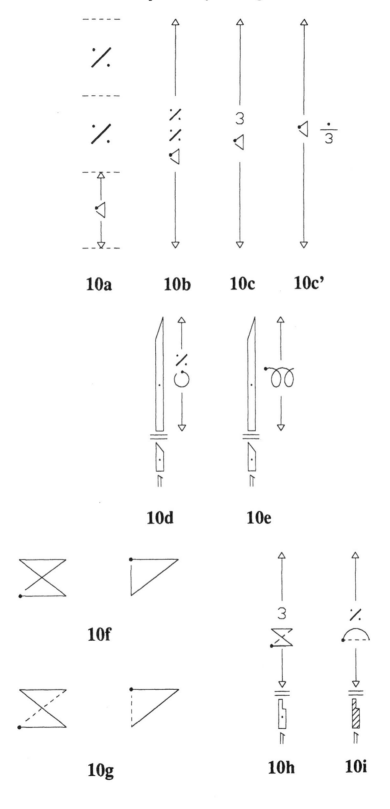

10a   10b   10c   10c'

10d   10e

10f

10g   10h   10i

10.5. If the limb travels while making a design, and the shape of the pattern takes the limb away from the stated path, as in **10j**, the limb must return to the general movement path each time, thus some 'retracing' is assumed. The retracing will be performed with less emphasis so that the pattern can be seen clearly.

10.6. The design may 'back-track' on the main path of a movement; this causes a break in the flow of the movement progression, but does not alter the general direction of the progression. Ex. **10l** illustrates the progression of **10k**.
   The general progression of the arm is upwards while the general progression of each design drawing is downwards. At the end of the movement, the arm must therefore be raised enough so that on completion of the fourth drawing the arm points to diagonal high and not lower. See understood starting point of design, section 15.

10.7. In **10m** the arm moves twice to a new location after performing the stated design. At each location the design is redrawn.

11   Surfaces

11.1. Most design drawing is experienced as a movement leaving a mark on an imaginary surface in the air, comparable to writing on a wall, drawing a design on a table top, on the ceiling, etc. This section explores in some detail the possible locations of design surfaces because some people experience difficulty in visualizing these surfaces.

11.2. Tracing a design is achieved most comfortably in front of the body, as if drawing on a blackboard, **11a**. For the moment let us take a design being drawn by the right arm (hand).

11.3. In writing on a blackboard in front of you, the design can move vertically (up and down) and laterally (from side to side); it is usually a combination of both.

11.4. An everyday example of such a situation for design drawing could be cleaning a window with a rag, during which figure-eights (or other patterns) could be made. The surface used is vertically in front of you.

11.5. In polishing a table, the surface is horizontally in front of the performer underneath the moving hand, **11b**. The design is moving sagittally (forward and backward) and laterally (side to side) on a horizontal surface.

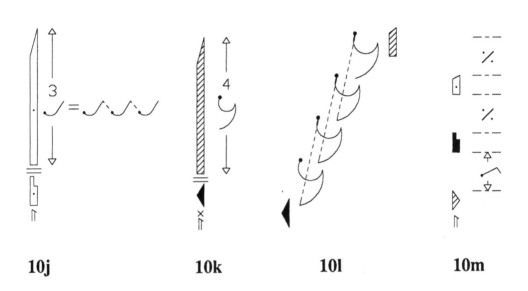

10j   **10k**   **10l**   **10m**

11a

11b

11.6. In winding a ball of wool, **11c**, or in cranking an old-fashioned gramophone, **11d**, the circular movement is in the sagittal plane combining forward and backward motion with up and down.

11.7. If a movement such as **11c** or **11d** were written as a design for the right arm, the surface on which the design is drawn would be at the left of the moving arm, as though one were facing the narrow edge of a door and drawing on the door's flat surface, **11e**. In this case the imagined surface is vertically to the left of the hand.

11.8. **Spatial orientation of surface.** In the various familiar actions of **11f-h** the shape in each example is the same (a circle), but it is placed differently in space. In winding a car window, **11f**, the design is 'drawn' on the 'wall' on the right; **11g**, which shows grinding coffee, is horizontal circling, as if on the floor, and **11h** shows waving a flag overhead, i.e. a circular design drawn as if on the ceiling.

11.9. To understand the idea of 'surface' on which the design is 'drawn', many people find the image of a sheet of paper with the design on it helpful. By holding this sheet up in the appropriate location they can see the surface and how the design takes place on it.

11.10. As this sheet is moved around, its placement in relation to the performer changes. Ex. **11i** illustrates the possible placement of the sheet in front of the performer, above the head (as if on the ceiling), on the floor, and at the intermediate situations of forward high and forward low.

11.11. In **11j** the sheet of paper is shown to be placed vertically to the right of the performer. In **11k** it is in the direction right side low.

11.12. Placements in diagonal directions are also possible. Ex. **11l** shows the surfaces which a three-sided mirror would provide.

11c

11d

11e

11f

11g

11h

11i

11j

11k

11l

12 Statement of Surface

12.1. Ex. **12a** is the sign for 'a surface'. [10] The flat edge can be said to represent the top of the sheet on which the design is drawn.

12.2. By placing the appropriate pin within this symbol a particular surface is designated. In **12b**, the surface is in front, as on a blackboard; in **12c** at your right, as on a wall to the right; in **12d** below, as on a table or the floor; and **12e** above, as if on the ceiling.

12.3. Use of high and low level pins indicate high or low placements. Ex. **12f** is forward low, as if writing on a slanted desk; **12g** is forward high as if on a sloping ceiling, while **12h** is side low, as though standing sideward in relation to the slanting desktop.

12.4. The sign for the surface is placed within the design path sign, before the indication of the design. In **12i-k** the same design is used, but the different placements describe different familiar actions. In **12i**, winding the wool is 'drawn' on the 'wall' on the left; **12j** is 'drawn' on the 'wall' on the right, and **12k** on the 'floor'. Ex. **12l** shows a figure-eight drawn on a slanting ceiling forward high of the 'writer'.

12.5. It is understood that in the following sections the term *surface* (of design) refers to the concept of 'surface' as used above to determine the orientation of designs and shapes in space, and not to an existing surface. In most cases there will not be a physical surface such as an actual wall or sheet of paper.

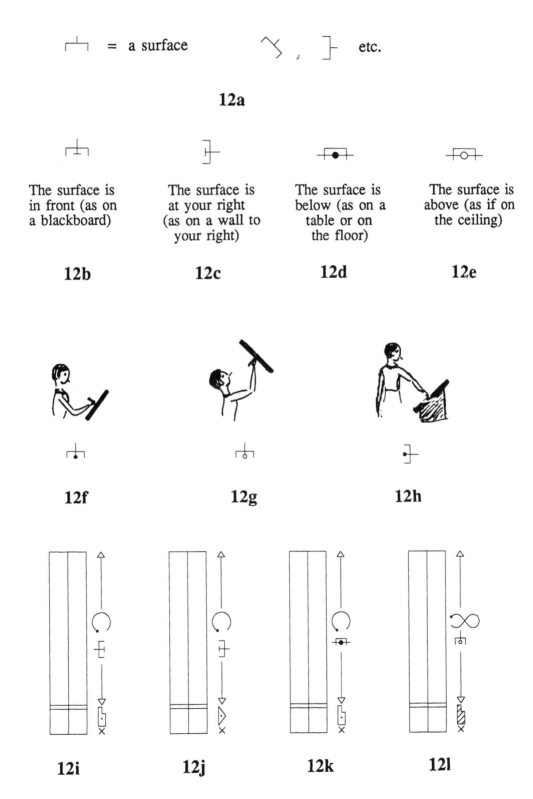

⌐⊓ = a surface   ↘ , ⊢ etc.

12a

The surface is in front (as on a blackboard)

The surface is at your right (as on a wall to your right)

The surface is below (as on a table or on the floor)

The surface is above (as if on the ceiling)

12b   **12c**   **12d**   **12e**

12f   **12g**   **12h**

12i   **12j**   **12k**   **12l**

13 Range of Possible Situations for a Surface

13.1. Ex. **13a** shows a bird's-eye view of different locations for the 'surface' (the sheet of paper) in front of the performer. The arm direction stated in the notation shows which placement is intended.

13.2. In **13b** the surface, which is to the left, is shown in several possible locations. Again, statement of arm direction indicates which placement is intended.

13.3. A commonly used 'surface' - the floor - need not literally be the floor itself, but may be a surface under the limb performing the design. In **13c** the design is under the right hand at each location of the arm. As stated above, the arm direction indicates the intended placement.

13.4. Exs. **13d-e** illustrate how the same design written with the same surface sign may take place in different actual locations in space. Ex. **13d** shows the palm of the right hand tracing two circles in the air on the forward surface. The palm itself must face forward. The circles are drawn to the right of the performer because of the preceding arm movement to the side. In **13e** the same circles are drawn in front of the performer because the arm moved there before design drawing.

  In these examples the fact that the right palm is facing forward is implied in the design indication (14.3). Explicit indication of palm facing may be added for clarification.

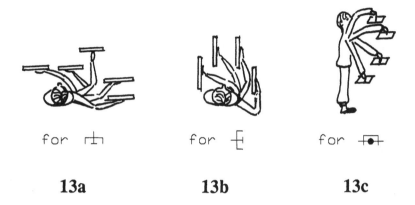

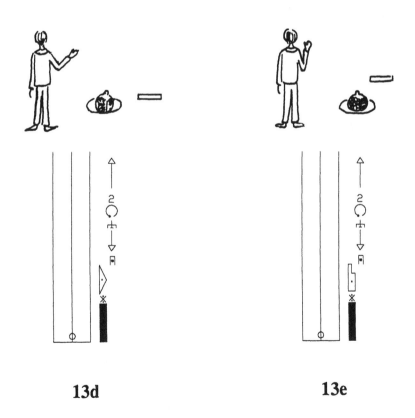

14 Clarification: Understood Orientation of Tracing Limb

14.1. **Understood surface.** Ex. **14a** illustrates what is the understood surface of a design if no surface is specifically indicated.

14.2. If the design is written for a limb or part of a limb, the surface of the design is understood to be at right angles to the shaft of that body part. In **14a** the imaginary surface is visualised as a sheet of paper.

14.3. If the design is written for a body surface, that body surface faces the design surface. In **14b** a design of the palm of the right hand is made on a surface directly in front of the performer. The palm is facing forward. This can be written (**14b'**) or left implied.

14.4. For clarity, the understood surface may be specifically indicated, as in **14c**.

14.5. **Performance on other (stated) surfaces.** The following examples involve designs drawn on surfaces other than that at a right angle to the shaft of the limb. The surface is not understood and therefore needs to be stated by a surface sign. In **14d** the arms start sideward and the circular design for the wrists (lower arms) is to be drawn as if on a forward middle surface. The wrists describe large circles the centre of which are the elbows. Halfway through the movement the hands are close to the shoulders.

To accomplish this movement the elbows remain out to the sides of the body while folding and unfolding completely. Some arm rotation is needed in addition. Compare with **14e**.

14.6. If the lower arms first move forward, **14e**, smaller circles will be traced in front of the elbows. It must be emphasized that **14d** cannot be used to mean the same as **14e**, i.e. if the lower arms are to move forward before the design drawing begins this must be explicitly stated.

14.7. From the starting position in these examples it is possible to have the wrists describe small circles while keeping the arms generally pointing out to the sides. This is achieved by arm flexion in which the elbows drop slightly each time the wrists move toward the body, and is written with a *surface* sign such as the one for the front of the wrist joint used in **14f**. Similar small wrist circles could also be accomplished by shifting the shoulder (i.e. displacing it in relation to the rest of the torso), with or without elbow flexion (cf. **14i** below). This last possibility is less expected.

A *surface* indication is needed in **14f** because designs written with the unqualified

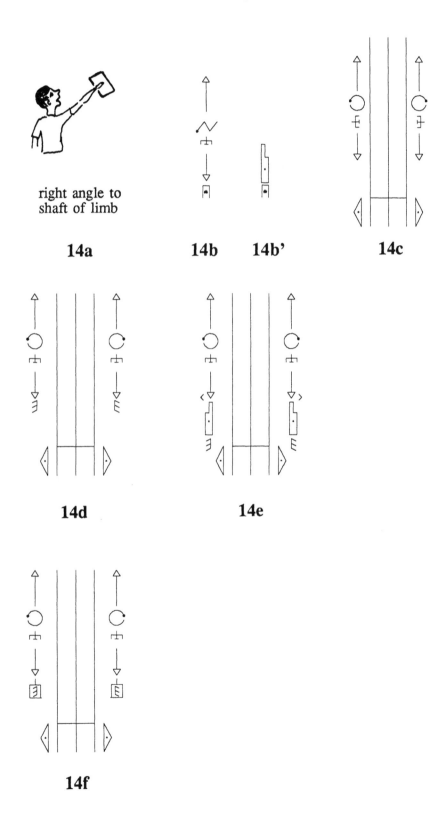

right angle to
shaft of limb

14a   **14b**   **14b'**   **14c**

14d   **14e**

14f

wrist sign are design paths of the lower arm and occur mainly through elbow flexion (previously explained in 6.2; cf. 7.2 and 33.17 (**33s**)).

14.8. Exs. **14g-i** are further examples making the same points as **14d-f**. They are concerned with hand and palm design on a side surface. The hand design of **14g** occurs chiefly in the wrist joint. The design is achieved by marked wrist flexion combined with lower arm rotation. The lower arm is not displaced in space. In **14h** there is no appreciable flexion in the wrist joint; the movement occurs mainly through elbow flexion (the elbow dropping towards the floor and then returning). The palm remains facing the right side surface throughout. In **14i** a small circular movement similar to that of **14h** is achieved not by elbow flexion but by shifting the shoulder. The arm is displaced as a fixed unit but the design is experienced as being traced by the palm of the hand.

15 Clarification: Starting Point of Design

15.1. In Motif Description, the exact starting point of the design in space is unknown unless the position of the tracing body part at the beginning of the design is stated in the notation, and the design can be conveniently drawn from that position.

Otherwise it is understood that the performer chooses the starting point of a design in such a way that all design drawing instructions can be respected.

15.2. In **15a** no specific starting point is given. The design is to be a very large square traced on the front surface. To achieve this the arm must first move to the area left forward in front of the performer. In other words, the arm performs an unemphasized preparatory gesture moving to a convenient starting point so that the whole design 'fits' on the stated surface. This gesture occurs just before the stated design tracing (in the upbeat to the design tracing).

15.3. In Structured Description, if the preparatory gesture is large and/or takes an appreciable amount of time, it is preferable to write it, as in **15b**.

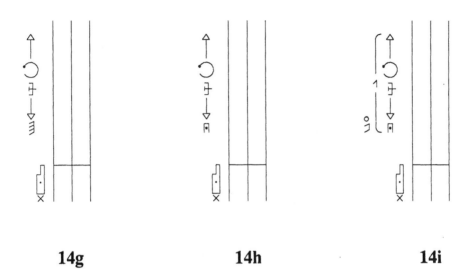

14g   **14h**   **14i**

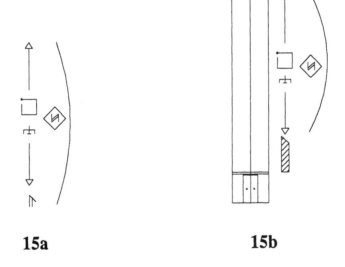

15a   **15b**

16 Placement of Design for 'Ceiling' and 'Floor'

16.1. In **16a**, a letter 'M' has been written on a sheet, the top of the sheet being clearly marked with a black line. In order to determine exactly how a design such as this 'M' should be traced, we need to know not only where the imaginary sheet (the surface) is located but also which way it is turned.[11] The expected orientation of the paper is as in ordinary reading. If the page is horizontal the top is forward. If the page is vertically placed the top is uppermost. On the forward middle surface in ex. **16b** the top naturally points upwards. When the sheet is moved clockwise, this orientation does not change.

16.2. In the progression of **16c**, the top of the sheet points to backward high when the sheet is held forward high, upward when the sheet is forward middle, forward high when the sheet is forward low and forward when the sheet is on the floor.

16.3. These are expected orientations. However, a question arises when the sheet is on the floor. Comparison of **16d** with **16e** shows that the top of a sheet on the floor could just as well point to the side, or any other direction. The same problem applies to sheets imagined on the ceiling.

16.4. Thus in the 'floor' and 'ceiling' situations for the 'surface' there is more than one possibility for placement of the design. The required orientation is in these cases specified by the choice of surface sign. This is illustrated in exs. **16e-g**. The flat edge of the surface sign can be said to represent the top of the 'paper' on which the design is drawn. In these examples, the sheet of paper with the 'M' on it is turned to tally with the appropriate surface sign.

16.5. **Adjustment of design.** Rather than adjusting placement of the sheet of paper to determine how to perform the design, the indication of the design itself can be changed, for example, instead of the sideward placement of **16h**, the design could be seen as **16i** in which the M is drawn sideways rather than the sheet of paper being turned. Instead of **16j**, a diagonal placement could be written as **16k**.

16.6. **Relation between 'ceiling' and 'floor' surfaces.** Drawing the 'M' on the ceiling, as in **16l**, for which one needs to look upward, could as well be drawn on a 'floor' surface, in which case the instruction would be **16m**. The limb may be up, overhead, but the image followed (and therefore possibly the performer's gaze, as in this illustration) may be below. Note the reversed image of the letter M in **16m**; the movement produced is the same as in **16l**. Cf. relation between front and back surfaces, **17i-k**.

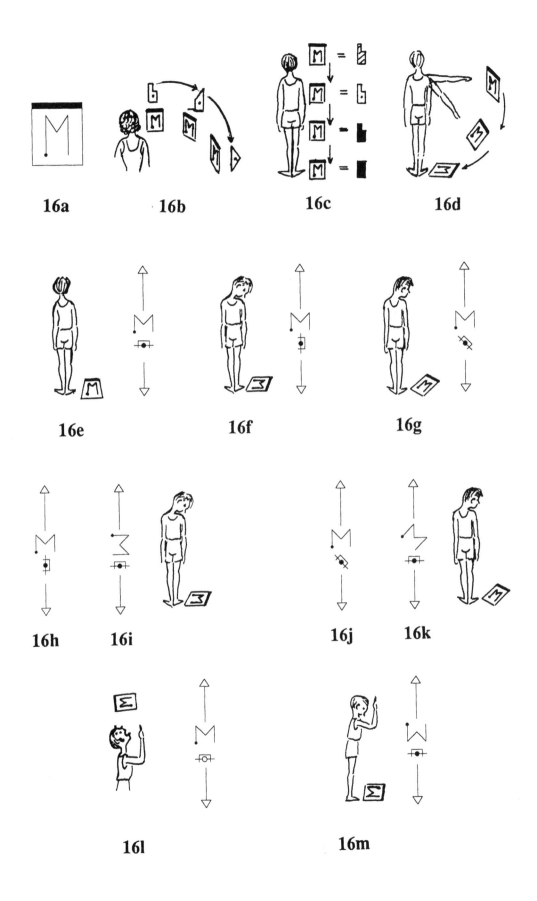

16a

16b

16c

16d

16e

16f

16g

16h

16i

16j

16k

16l

16m

17 Determining Surface Behind the Body

17.1. Because much Design Drawing is concerned with pantomimic gestures and these occur usually within the front hemisphere of the kinesphere, it is rare for a design to be drawn on a surface behind the body. However, should such an instance occur, one must know how it should be written and read.[12]

17.2. The natural inclination is to direct the eyes comfortably toward the surface of the design, rather than to bend backward or to trace without looking. Let us consider a housepainter working on the walls and ceiling of a room. He will face the surface to be painted whenever possible. He will paint the ceiling for instance as though 1/4 somersault backward had occured. Thus the sheet of paper, previously situated in front of him, will have been subjected to 1/4 backward revolution when it is imagined on the ceiling, as in **17a**. For these examples the direction sign of the active arm and the most appropriate surface sign are given with each figure illustration, **17b** etc.
See also **16l-m**.

17.3. If our man has to paint behind him, as in **17c**, it is likely he will twist his body to the right or left while his feet on the ladder will keep their original front (Stance).
The design will be physically at the right side of the painter's shoulder line. This right side direction is the standard arm direction when twisting the body, **17d**, and so will usually be the writer's choice. A side surface sign is used in this case.
The design, situated on the 'back wall', is backward in relation to Stance, **17e**. If this key is chosed, the surface sign to be used is the backward one.
In general, the Standard Key is used unless there is a special reason for selecting the Stance Key.

17.4. **Stance description.** In certain cases it is more appropriate to use a Stance description, perhaps when the same design is repeated in different directions around the performer.

17.5. In **17f**, the design is located right side high for the arm, backward high in relation to the untwisted front (Stance), **17g**. The usual choice of description would be as in **17h**.

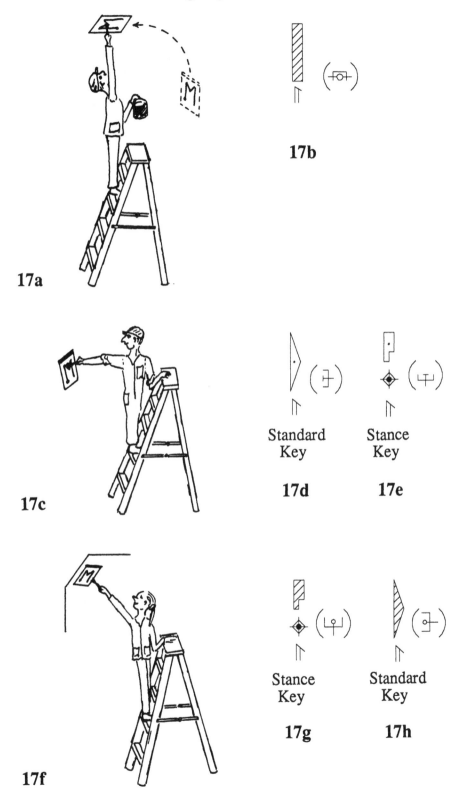

17a

17b

17c

Standard
Key

17d

Stance
Key

17e

17f

Stance
Key

17g

Standard
Key

17h

17.6. **Relation between 'front' and 'back' surfaces.** When no body twist occurs, a design which appears to be on a back surface can just as well be drawn as an image on a front surface, performed like a mirror image. Ex. **17i** describes the design of someone penciling in eyebrows, first the right, then the left. If a long pencil is used, as in the illustration, the other end of the pencil points into the forward direction and traces the design as it is written in the notation. The surface is followed as seen in the mirror rather than painted on the face. Note that the indication of **17i** should be part of a more elaborate notation recording the placement of the arm and hand including the direction in which the fingers point, and contact with or proximity to the eyebrows. On its own, the indication of **17i** would cause the reader to trace the design, as it is written, in front of him, fingers pointing towards the front.

17.7. A similar case is illustrated in **17j** in which the design, here the letter P, is being drawn mirror-fashion on the performer's chest. The hand drawing the letter is following the image of a letter P as if displayed on a card held in front of the performer.

17.8. To produce a true letter P on the chest, as in **17k**, the performer must use a reverse image in the mirror.

17.9. For exs. **17i-k** there is of course a choice between description in relation to the front or to the back surface, as shown for **17k**.

17.10. Ex. **17l** illustrates a design drawn behind the head, a spiral pattern as in applying shampoo while washing the hair. The action, the design, is imagined as being drawn on a forward low surface.

18 State of Limb in Design Drawing

18.1. When designs such as the letter 'M', a figure-eight, etc. are drawn on a wall in front, the arm can be held more or less extended all the time, **18a**. If the 'wall' is closer and the arm is bent to start with, it can remain in that state of flexion.

18.2. But if the same design is drawn on a 'table top,' the arm must flex and extend to follow the line of the letter, **18b**.

18.3. The degree of such flexion and extension for **18b** will depend on the size of the design and how near or far it is. The limb may begin quite flexed and then merely flex less and then more, etc.

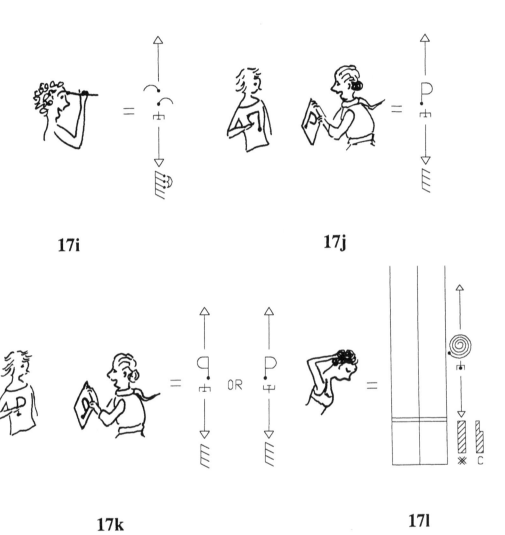

17i   **17j**

17k   **17l**

18a   **18b**

18.4. *Flexion and extension of the tracing limb is understood* when dictated by other circumstances such as proximity and size of the design. It can be explicitly stated in the usual way if needed, cf. **22b**.

See also distance of design surface, section 21.

19   Shape of Surface

19.1. So far we have spoken of the surface as being flat - a wall, desktop, etc. - but it may also be curved. In many instances the shape of the surface on which a design is drawn may not be important, but in some pantomimic gestures there is a clear need for an obviously flat or curved surface to be indicated.

19.2. When a design is drawn with an extended limb and no flexion occurs, because of the build of the shoulder socket the extremity will move on a curve, a concave surface as if drawing on the inside of a sphere, **19a-c**. This is not noticeable unless the design is large.

19.3. Specific use of a flat surface requires some flexion at the appropriate points, **19d-f**.

19.4. Even more flexion is needed for drawing on convex surfaces, as in drawing around a large globe, **19g-i**. It is particularly for these cases that the need arises to indicate the shape of the surface. Recording the changes in flexion or extension for the limb can be intricate and does not convey what is most important, i.e. the shape of the surface.

19.5. Ex. **19j** is the indication for 'a surface' (introduced in 12.1), the shape of which is not specified. This is the indication most commonly used, since so often the shape of the surface is unimportant. Ex. **19k** indicates a curved surface; no particular kind is specified. Ex. **19l** specifies a flat surface, while **19m** states a convex surface and **19n** a concave one.[13]

19.6. Whatever the shape of the surface, it may be close to the body or farther away. In an arm design, the nearer the surface is to the body, the more the arm will bend to produce the design on the stated surface. See also section 21.

19.7. Ex. **19o**, in which a flag is waved overhead, is an interesting example since it makes no difference whether the surface is designated as curved or flat.

19.8. However, in **19p** the zig-zag design which moves across the top of the kinesphere will naturally use a slightly curved surface since the arm remains normally extended. There is no need to stipulate a curved surface.

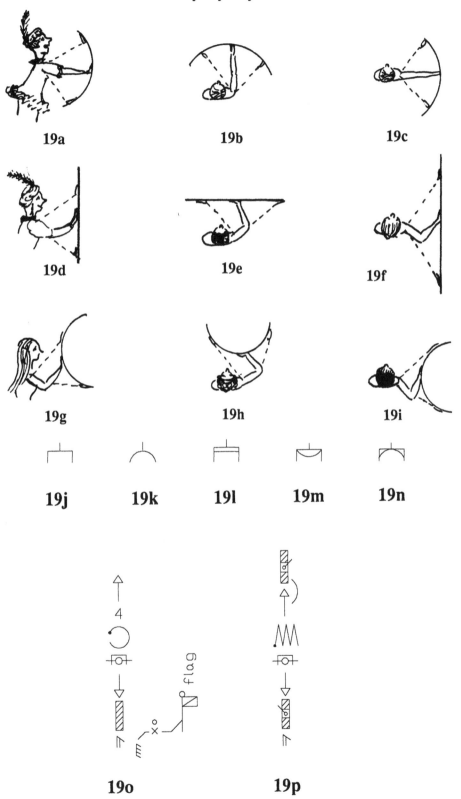

19a

19b

19c

19d

19e

19f

19g

19h

19i

19j

19k

19l

19m

19n

19o

19p

19.9. In **19q** a large performance of the design is specified as well as a concave surface. The movement begins and ends with a bent arm. To perform this the arm must extend slightly half-way through each stroke and flex slightly more at the end of each stroke.

19.10. In **19r**, where the arm begins and ends extended, the same design is performed on a flat surface. The arm needs to flex in the middle of each stroke. The necessary flexion is taken for granted and not written (see 18.4). If important, exact degrees of flexion/extension can be stated.

20   Surfaces - Charts

20.1. For those who enjoy or are helped by organized charts the following illustrations are provided. The charts are drawn from bird's-eye view.

20.2. Location of the eight main horizontal surfaces around the body is indicated by use of the appropriate pin. In the following illustrations both curved and flat surfaces are specified.

20.3. Ex. **20a** shows the eight horizontal concave 'surfaces' around the body. In **20b** these surfaces are shown as flat and in **20c** as convex. Though rarely used, convex surfaces need to be considered and hence indication for them is provided.

20.4. Please note that, as explained in section 13, surfaces are not necessarily opposite the performer's body, as is the case with the surfaces shown in these charts. When the body is twisted, surfaces relate to the front of the twisted body section, unless a Stance Key is used. Thus their situation changes with each body twist (previously explained in 17.3).
  As mentioned before, the three surfaces behind the body are rarely used.

20.5. Each of the surfaces illustrated in **20a-c** can also be at a high or low level. Exs. **20d-f** illustrate (in a bird's-eye view, as though the sphere were opened out and flattened) the range of surfaces in front and to the side of the body. Ex. **20d** shows the concave surfaces, **20e** the flat surfaces, and **20f** the convex surfaces.
  These charts do not include the 'ceiling' and 'floor' surfaces (cf. section 16).

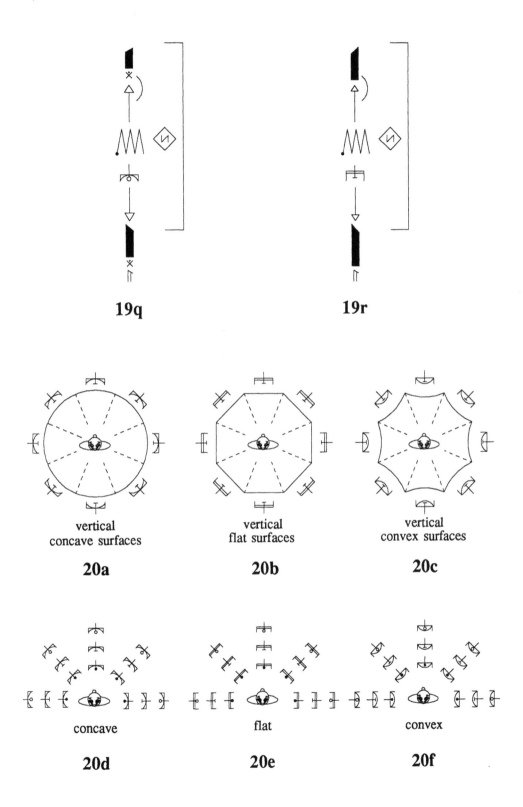

19q

19r

vertical
concave surfaces

20a

vertical
flat surfaces

20b

vertical
convex surfaces

20c

concave

20d

flat

20e

convex

20f

21 Distance of Surface from Performer

21.1. A design drawn with the arm extended as in **21a** could be drawn in an identical fashion closer to the body as in **21b** if arm flexion is indicated. In **21a** and **21b** parallel surfaces are being used, indicated by the same surface sign.

21.2. The image traced (real or imaginary) could be seen or imagined some distance away. In **21c** the design in a picture on the wall is being drawn by the index finger. The distance between performer and picture has no bearing on the notation: only the actual body action is notated.

22 Displacement During Design Drawing

22.1. As discussed briefly in 9.5 (**9d**), the limb or part of the body may travel in space while a pattern is being drawn. This displacement may be movement into another direction, or it may involve limb flexion or extension.

22.2. Ex. **22a** shows the arm tracing a zig-zag design while moving from one diagonal to another, the exact displacement being indicated by the direction symbols. Ex. **22b** shows arm extension occuring while tracing a similar design; the arm ends stretched.

22.3. **Change of front.** If the performer turns while drawing a design, it is understood that the surface on which the design is 'drawn' turns with him/her, keeping the same relationship to the front of the performer, as illustrated in **22c**.

22.4. **Design and whole body displacement.** In **22d** a half turn with steps in place occurs while a vertical (downward and up) zig-zag design is being drawn. As a result of the turning, the pattern covers more space, being stretched out laterally in the direction of the turn.

22.5. In certain cases there is a clear choice between drawing the actual spatial displacement of the tracing body part, or drawing the design according to a mental image. In other words, the notation may

(1) represent the actual trace pattern as it occurs in space, regardless of which aspect of the movement is a result of design drawing and which is caused by traveling or turning of the body or body part

(2) represent the design as it would be done if no turn or displacement of the body occured. (See examples overleaf).

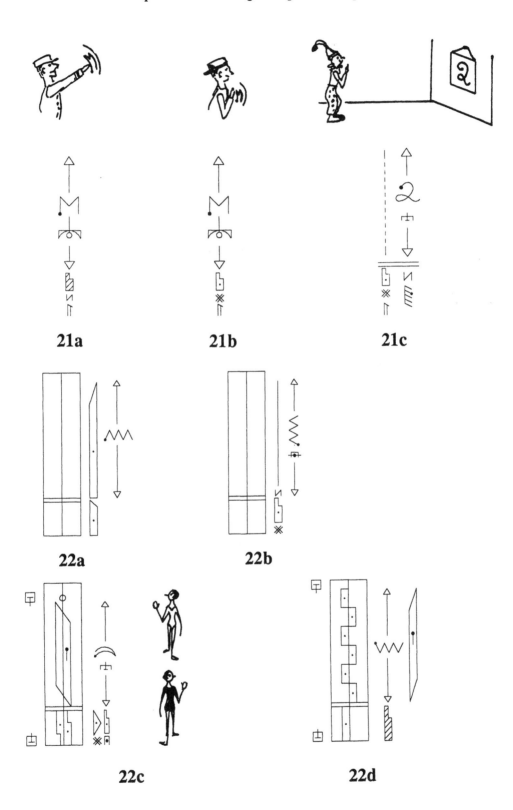

21a   **21b**   **21c**

22a   **22b**

22c   **22d**

22.6. Ex. **22e** is an example of the first method and is similar to **22a** or **22b**. Ex. **22f** exemplifies the second method: the displacement results from the extension indication, and the circular movement from the design path. Exs. **22e** and **22f** produce the same thing, but they give a different image. Depending on the case one image may be more appropriate than the other. See also **10d-e**.

22.7. In actual practice, ambiguity is rare. In **22g** the direction of travel and the direction in which the design progresses are in opposition. A resultant direction for the right arm should be indicated if it is imperative that the right arm becomes more extended as a result of the steps.

22.8. In the unlikely event that it is unclear which method is used, as a rule the design indication itself should be read as if no simultaneous rotation or displacement took place (method (2) in 22.9 above).

22.9. **Retention of surface.** When the performer turns a small amount, the surface on which the design is drawn may remain static, i.e. not turn, as when a teacher turns slightly away from the blackboard to address the class while continuing to write. The situation of the design and the surface used change in relation to the performer, but not in relation to space.

22.10. In **22h** the writer is facing the wall. Ex. **22i** shows that the writer has turned 1/4 to the right at the end of drawing the design, but the surface has not adjusted spatially. While this example illustrates a tangible surface, the same can occur with an imaginary one.

22.11. A space hold is used above the surface sign as in **22j** to indicate such retention in space. The imaginary design travels but does not turn with the performer; at the beginning the surface is in front, at the end to his/her left.

22.12. In **22k** the direction of progression of the arm design is contrary to that of the performer's turn. The arm starts across the body. The design is drawn on the 'surface' at the left which has a spatial retention, thus becoming, as the performer turns, a surface in front and then a surface to the performer's right. The arm ends to the right of the body. This can be specified by direction symbols for the arm. In this example, the arm movement is understood: only the design is specified. Movement occurs in the shoulder joint as a result of the space hold. In addition, the hand is displaced in the clockwise direction because of the design pattern.

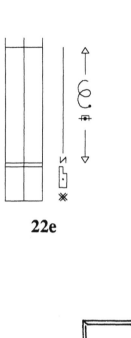

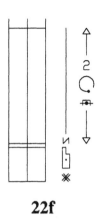

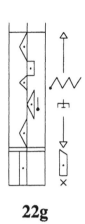

22e   **22f**   **22g**

22h   **22i**

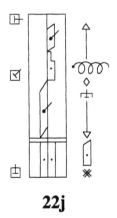

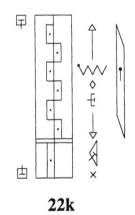

22j   **22k**

23 Change of Surface

23.1. A design may start on one surface and then change to another, giving a three-dimensional effect. This can be shown on one diagram by a small dotted line through the design line indicating the moment of change of surface, the new surface being written alongside as in **23a** in which an initially vertical curve ends as a horizontal curve.

23.2. Or a shape may be broken up into segments with the new surface stated between each, as in **23b**. It is, however, preferable to draw the shape in one continuous design where possible.

Note: Many curving patterns written in this way may, strictly speaking, produce a slight 'break', resulting in an angle at the point of changing surface. For general purposes, this can be ignored if the angle is not particularly sharp and the overall design is curved, rounded. In specific notation supplementary indications can be added if either an angle or a continuous curve is to be stressed.

23.3. Ex. **23c** provides another example in which one semi-circle is drawn on a surface 'below' (as on the floor), then another semi-circle on the surface vertically in front. In **23d** a circular pattern is shown to repeat through use of repeat signs, next to which is placed the change of surface for each repeat.

24 Intermediate Surfaces[14]

24.1. Intermediate surfaces can be distinguished and stated by combining the appropriate pins in the surface sign.

24.2. Ex. **24a** shows a semi-circular design on a horizontal surface (as on the floor). In **24b** the surface used is that between that of **24a** and **24c**, the forward low surface. In **24d** the surface is halfway between that of **24c** and **24e**, the forward surface. Ex. **24f** shows all five surfaces, **24b** and **24d** being indicated by dotted lines.

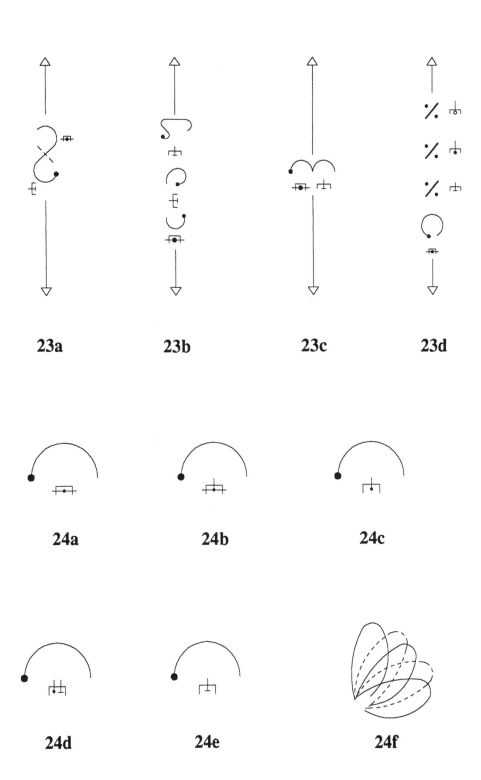

23a   23b   23c   23d

24a   24b   24c

24d   24e   24f

25 Deviations from the Surface

25.1. A deviation from the plane of the design, that is, from the usual line of the design, can produce a three-dimensional design. This may be indicated by appropriate use of a pin. Such a deviation relates to the line of the path of the movement, just as pins within vertical bows indicate deviations from the line of a movement written with direction symbols. More than one deviation may occur and the deviations may be irregular. The first example is again the semi-circular design on a horizontal surface, **25a**.

25.2. In **25b** a pin representing the deviation is placed next to the centre of the design and is understood to be spread evenly throughout the design from start to finish.

25.3. However, a deviation may appear at different points on the path of the design. In the following illustrations, a straight line is used to simplify the drawings. Below each illustration is given the application of each variation to the design of **25a**. Note use of dotted lines to indicate where the deviation starts and finishes.

25.4. In **25c** there is a slight, momentary rise in the middle of the design.

25.5. Ex. **25d**: a slight rise at the start of the design; **25e**, a slight rise at the end.

25.6. Ex. **25f**: a rise during the first half of the path; **25g**, a rise during the second half of the path.

25.7. An asymmetrical deviation which takes effect at the beginning is illustrated in **25h**; **25i** shows an asymmetrical deviation which takes effect at the end. The pins are like magnets exerting greater deviation on the part of the path they are nearest and less on the rest of the path.

25.8. The idea and the writing rules explained in this section follow the same logic as ordinary deviations from the line of the path of a movement.

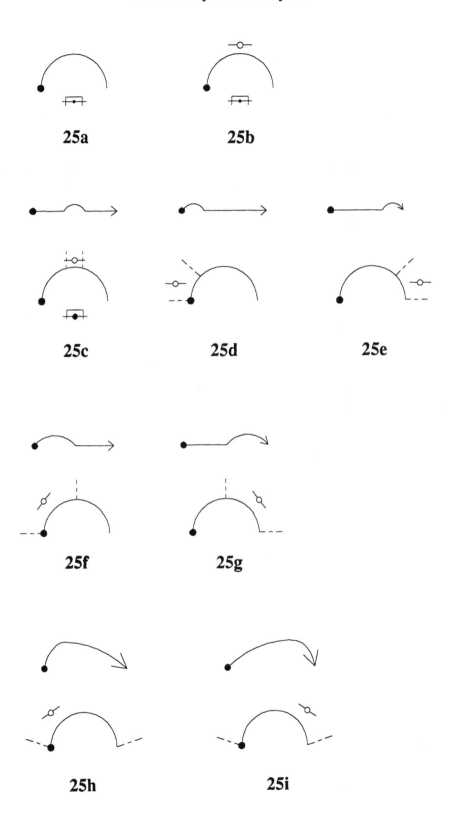

25a

25b

25c

25d

25e

25f

25g

25h

25i

26 Deviations for an Angular Design

26.1. Pins can also be used for deviations in other kinds of designs. Ex. **26a** shows a basic vertical design placed on the forward middle surface.

26.2. When two deviations are shown, the return to the plane of the stated surface is understood to occur halfway between them. In **26b** the first rising movement will deviate a little forward; on the second rising movement, the 'peak' will deviate slightly backward of the stated plane, i.e. toward the performer. The design ends on the vertical plane on which it started. The path of the design deviates from the stated plane but the design consists nevertheless of straight lines.

26.3. In **26c** a forward deviation occurs on the first upward stroke, and a backward deviation on the last downward stroke; the remainder of the design is on the stated plane. Note use of the dotted lines to indicate to what part of the design the deviation pin refers. The path of the first and last sections of the design become curved because of the deviation.

26.4. **Two of the same deviations.** A scallop pattern can be made by two of the same deviations, the design returning to the plane in between, as in **26d**, in which there are two forward scallops on the way up and two backward ones on the way down.

26.5. The even, curved deviations of **26e** could be described in the setting of **26f** in which the design is drawn on the left surface while the arm travels to the right. As a result of the arm moving, the design is "opened up" when viewed from the side. It is from this viewpoint, taken in **26f**, that the deviations are most apparent.

26.6. **Retention of deviation.** If a deviation from the stated path is to be retained for a while, i.e. traveling 'on the deviation', two of the same pins arc used without any dotted line separating them, **26g**. After the second pin, a return to the plane is understood. A sideward view of **26g** would be as **26h**, a design drawn on the left surface during which the arm travels to the right.

26.7. Two more variations: a wavy line is produced by **26i**, using first a downward, then an upward deviation. In **26j** a design on the forward middle surface curves first forward, then backward on the way up, and first backward and then forward on the way down.

26.8. A similarly subtle pattern is given in **26k**. In a design drawn 'on the floor' the deviation is first diagonally forward, then diagonally backward while still progressing on the forward path.

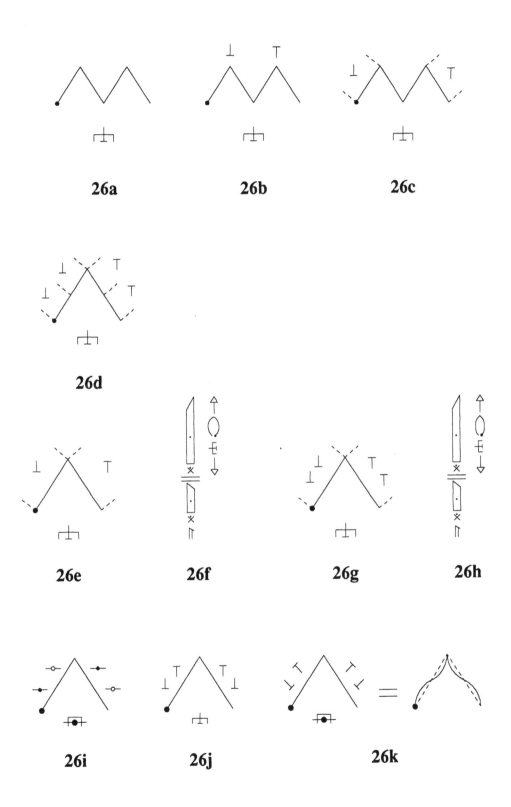

26a

26b

26c

26d

26e

26f

26g

26h

26i

26j

26k

27 Degree of Deviation

27.1. Degree of deviation can be specified by using space measurement signs as shown in **27a-c**. These measurement signs are placed next to the pin indicating the deviation. They modify the *design*: there is no question of reference to flexion and extension of limbs.[15]

27.2. In **27a** there is only a very slight rise on the semi-circular design.

27.3. In **27b** a relatively large rising deviation occurs on the forward part of the pattern, a less high deviation on the backward part of the inverted 'V' shape.

27.4. In **27c** scallops of downward deviations are of different sizes. In **27d** the dotted line is the basic design, and the solid line shows the four downward scallops.

In **27d** the performer is standing on the right of the drawing facing to the left. The movement is viewed from the performer's left side.

27.5. When the design is large enough and spatially simple, a better description of the movement may well be of ordinary gestures modified by deviations, e.g. **27b** might be written as **27e**.

27.6. As can be seen, much detail can be added. The shape within the design path can be drawn as large as need be to accommodate the details. In a score a simplified version can be given with an enlarged version placed nearby or in a glossary. In detailed notation it is likely that placement of the limb and other movement factors written in the columns in the usual way will modify the design and provide specific details of performance.

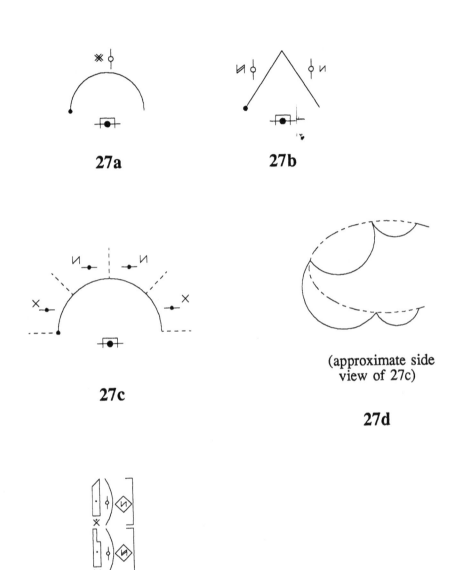

27a

27b

27c

(approximate side
view of 27c)

27d

27e

II. FORMING A BODY SHAPE

A static shape to be formed by positioning the body, parts of the body, or by more than one body, is often based on recognizable, established designs. Though the body is three-dimensional in build it can, in terms of expression, produce a one-dimensional (linear), two-dimensional (planal) or three-dimensional (plastic, global) shape.

28 Representation of Shape

28.1. The visible, static shape to be made by the performer is drawn as pictorially as possible. Exs. **28a-i** illustrate familiar possibilities.

28.2. To state that the design indicated represents a static shape and is not a notation symbol or other indication, the sign for 'shape' (previously introduced as **1b**) is placed before the appropriate shape indication as in **28j-m**.
See also examples **36d, 37f-g**.

28.3. **Three-dimensional shape.** The sign for 'shape' can be modified by adding a vertical stroke as in **28n-p** to show three-dimensional shapes. Ex. **28n** shows a sphere, **28o** a lotus-like shape and **28p** a clockwise spiral. Spirals are difficult to represent pictorially on two-dimensional paper; if needed additional indications can specify it more exactly.

29 Part Forming the Shape

29.1. The appropriate body part sign is placed before the sign for 'shape' to indicate what part is to produce the stated shape.

29.2. In **29a** the torso makes an arc shape (half a circle). This may be achieved by bending forward, a common form of curving the spine.

29.3. In **29b** the back surface of head to pelvis as a unit forms a half circle.

29.4. Ex. **29c** shows an angular shape formed by the arm. The illustrations show possible ways of making this shape. The first illustration is seen from the performer's back and the second from his right side.

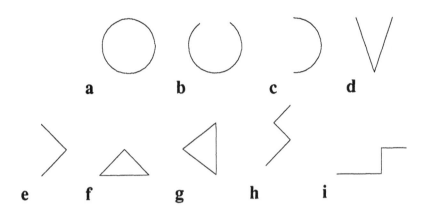

a   b   c   d

e   f   g   h   i

28a-i

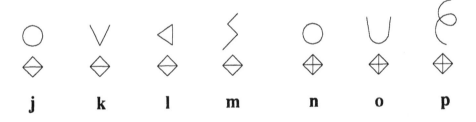

j   k   l   m   n   o   p

28j-p

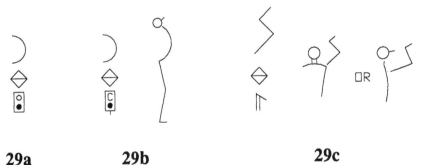

OR

29a   **29b**   **29c**

29.5. The shape for the right leg of **29d** might produce the position of **29e** or **29f**, though for **29f** the shape would better be drawn as in **29g**.

29.6. The hand position of **29h** will be produced with the thumb forming the line and the fingers the arc.

29.7. Ex. **29i** is the 'V' for victory sign made by the index and middle fingers. The palm facing eliminates the need to show indication of a surface for the shape.

29.8. Shapes using both hands may be written as in **29j** and **29k**. These examples allow for several possible performances. Compare with **29l** and **29m**.

29.9. **Shape combined with direction and surface.** There is often more than one setting in which a shape can be viewed and performed. The basic situation of the body as a whole or of the limb involved will usually be indicated, e.g. torso upright, tilted or lying down, or the placement of limbs in particular directions. Accompanying details can include from which side the shape is to be seen, that is, on which imaginary surface a shape is to be placed. Exs. **29l** and **29m** are determinate statements using the general indications of shape of **29j** and **29k**. The exact manner of performance is dictated by arm and hand directions and by surface signs. For a further example, see **32d**.

30 Indication of Timing

30.1. Duration of the movement which produces a body shape is shown by an action stroke; the formation of the shape is the aim, the end result, as in **30a** in which the hands make a heart shape.

30.2. In **30b** the shape is the result of a sudden action; both the sign for the right hand and the sign for shape have been placed before the double horizontal line to show that they are not counted in the timing. The addition of an accent sign also indicates the sharpness of the action. Note that the *hand* sign is used, as it is a shape of the hand as a whole and not just the fingers.

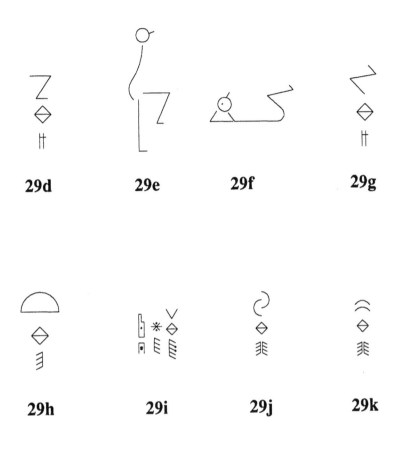

29d **29e** **29f** **29g**

29h **29i** **29j** **29k**

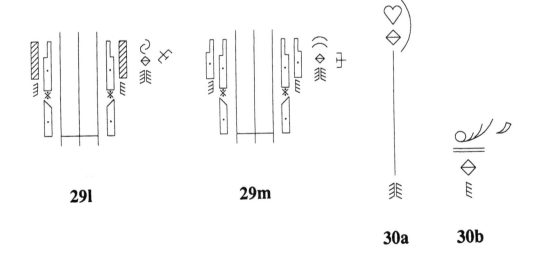

29l **29m**

30a **30b**

31 Validity

31.1. Duration of holding (maintaining) an established shape is shown in Motif Writing by the addition of a hold sign, as in **31a**. In Structured Description a gap (empty space) following the statement of the shape indicates the time during which this shape is maintained. However, if other movement indications occur which might or might not cancel the shape, a retention should be indicated for clarification.

31.2. Retention is usually expressed by a body hold, but a space hold or spot hold may be applicable in particular circumstances.

31.3. **Cancellation.** A shape is canceled by a decrease or a 'back to normal' sign (**31b**); by an action which obviously breaks the shape as in **31c**, in which the three-dimensional extension of the hands cancels the previous closed shape; or by indication of another shape. A decrease sign specifies that the shape disappears, while a 'back to normal' sign refers to the return to normal carriage for the part or parts of the body involved.[16]

32 Miscellaneous

32.1. When movement leading to establishing a shape needs to be written out in full, the desired shape may still be stated outside the staff, as in **32a**. Here the shape is written in parentheses to show the end result of the structured movement. As in the writing of language, such use of parentheses indicates an additional piece of information or a reminder.[17]

32.2. Another example of this is **32b** in which the arms make the shape of a heart, [18] taken from the Gigue in Doris Humphrey's *Partita*.

32.3. A trace design may be made by a part of the body which is itself making or holding a particular shape. In **32c** the left hand, held in the shape of a letter C, is describing an open circle in the sagittal plane (as if drawn on the wall at the left). The action is led by the fingertips so that a 'scooping' movement results.

32.4. In **32d** the thumb and fingers which are held in a very flat 'U' shape make a jagged design horizontally from left to right. Indication of surface helps

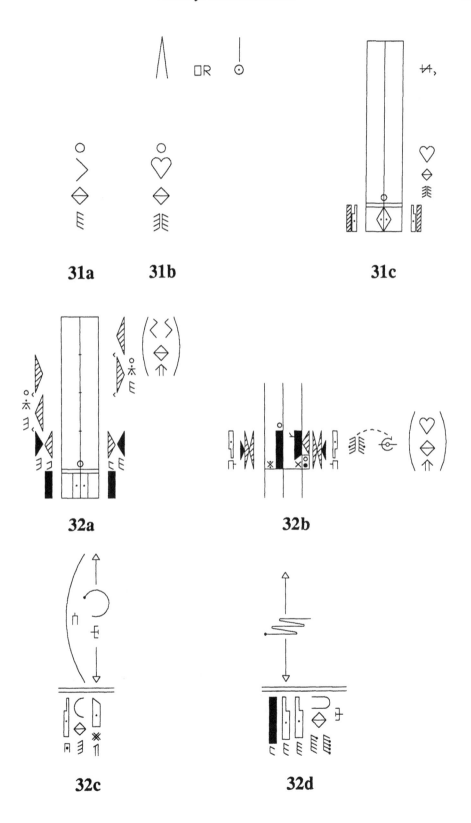

31a   31b   31c

32a   32b

32c   32d

to identify the orientation in space of the shape.

Because no surface is indicated for the *design*, this 'surface' is understood to be at right angles to the 'shaft' of the hand (cf. 14.2), in this case the front surface, thus the jagged pattern progresses to the right while slightly rising. The design involves movement in the elbow and shoulder joints.

III. READING EXAMPLES [19]

33 Trace Patterns for the Limbs and Their Parts

33.1. Ex. **33a** shows a fall ending in a lying position.[20] The arms make small circles while extended to the side, the familiar gesture of trying to recover balance and to keep the body from falling backward. The shift forward of the pelvic area also serves to keep the main body weight from moving backward.

For repeating the design path see section 10.

33.2. In **33b** the sagittal scooping movement of the arm is restated for clarification as a trace design of a half circle. The design path sign has no pre-sign; it is therefore understood to apply to the right arm as this is the only body part moving.

33.3. In **33c** a three-dimensional path is traced by the right arm. First the back of the hand, then the little finger edge is leading the gesture. The direction symbols and indications of parts leading describe the movement in detail. The design drawing indication is added so that the movement can immediately be visualized.

Change of surface in tracing design, see section 23, cf. also **33f**.

33.4. Ex. **33d** shows a pantomime gesture expressing the action of rubbing the stomach after swallowing an egg.[21] Hands circle in opposite directions. The right hand starts and ends below the left.

In the starting position, the palms of both hands are touching the front of the chest, elbows out to the sides. The sliding action ends with the left palm touching the waist in front and slightly to the left, and the right palm touching the pelvis in front and slightly to the right.

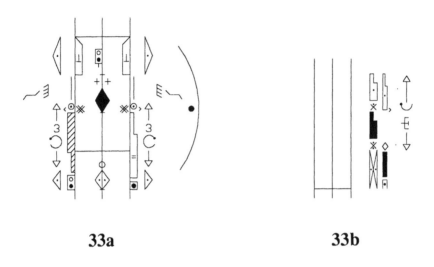

33a   **33b**

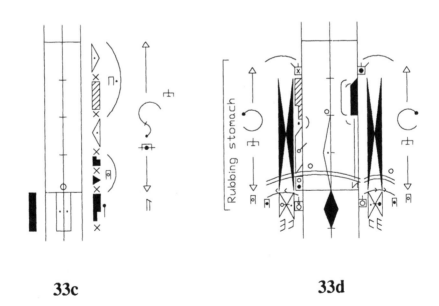

33c   **33d**

33.5. The arm gestures of **33e** are borrowed from Spanish dance.[22] While the performer bends progressively backwards the lower arms, rising in front of the body, circle around each other every two counts.

In this kind of design, care should be taken to have each arm start at the right point of the little circle of the design. The design path of the right lower arm is clockwise, that of the left anticlockwise. The overall effect, however, is of the hands circling around each other in the sagittal plane (as in a somersault roll of the whole body forward).

The torso contraction reached at the end, combined with the backward tilt, takes place over the back surface of the body. Repeats indicate each hand performs 3 circles while fingers snap alternately marking each count in the 3/4 metre.

33.6. Exs. **33f** and **33g** show different ways of bowing for men.

In **33f** the wrist (i.e. the lower arm) describes an S-like pattern the first half of which is written as on the floor and the second half as on a wall to the left.

For change of surface in tracing design, see section 23. Cf. also **33c**.

Ex. **33g** was originally a gesture made with hat in hand during a bow. The circular movement of the hand occurs chiefly in the wrist joint, although some involvement of the lower arm (elbow joint) is indicated. At the end of the movement the arm rotates outward to end palm up.

33.7. In the second measure of **33h** a circular movement of the right shoulder occurs.[23] Trace paths for the shoulder usually occur on the side middle surface of the same side, the movement consisting of shifting the shoulder out of alignment in relation to the rest of the chest area. In the score this movement is notated in the conventional way with four direction signs. Ex. **33h'** shows how the same movement can be described using design drawing.

In the third measure the hand makes a beckoning gesture that occurs mainly in the wrist joint and is amplified by a slight lifting of the arm and the rotation and participation of the forearm. The design path gives the immediate image of the hand circling 'over the top'. The exact description in terms of hand and wrist movement preclude ambiguity as to the manner of performance. Cf. **33t**.

33.8. Exs. **33i-j** show an exercise performed while lying on the back. The right leg is pointed towards the ceiling and then begins to describe increasingly large circles (an increasing spiral). The surface indication is not necessary but added for clarification. After 4 circles the performer changes legs to start on the other side. The exercise is done twice on each side.

In the design drawing of **33i** the increasing spiral appears pictorially. In the more conventional way of writing of **33j** the first very small circular leg movement is described with pins; this leg movement is then shown to be repeated

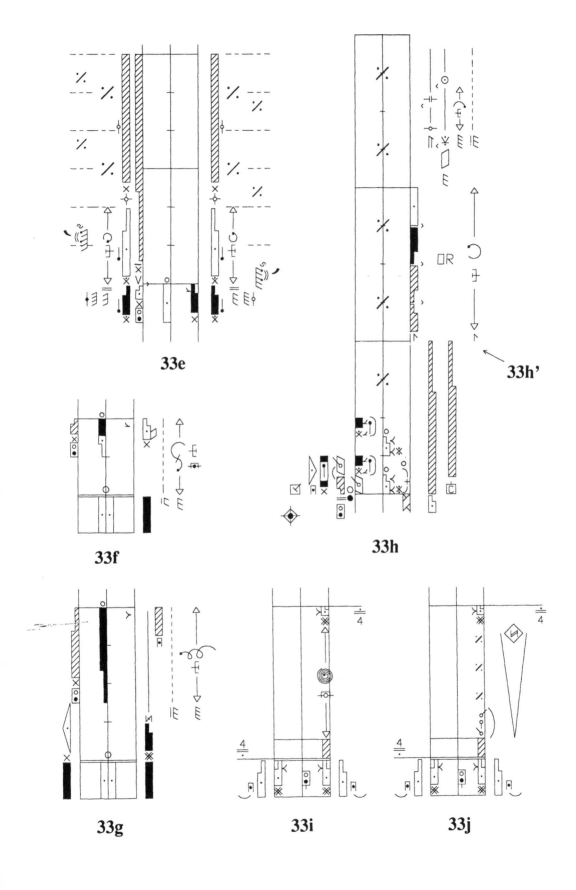

33e

33h'

33f

33h

33g

33i

33j

3 times more, a 'spatially large' symbol placed in an increase sign indicating the increasing spiral.

33.9. In **33k** the right ankle traces a continuous design of two circles and a figure-8 while remaining in contact with the floor (on the ball of the foot). The surface on which the design is drawn is therefore necessarily the floor. The design cannot, of course, be written as one *for the foot* because in that case the action would mainly take place in the ankle joint, the foot moving independently of the leg. This parallels the distinction established between *hand* and *wrist* designs, etc. (cf. 6.2).

The right thigh is shown to be excluded from the movement. This implies that the knee does not move in space. In moving the foot forward and backward the knee joint is used. In moving it in sideward directions one should not allow the thigh to move in space, although rotation will occur in the hip joint. Slight flexion at the ankle joint is needed to keep the ball of the foot on the floor.

For exclusion bow, see 7.6 (**7i**).

33.10. The series **33l-n** shows a curved design traced clockwise around the body, the design being augmented by the turn of the body. This gesture might be seen to express the idea of 'those hills over there'. The performer looks at the right hand. The little finger edge of the right hand is leading, causing the arm to rotate very slightly inward and outward. The examples denote very similar movements, each specifying different aspects.

In **33l** the size of the design is dictated by inclusion of the torso in the arm movements and by arm directions before and after the design drawing. These directions are written in the Stance key. Torso inclusion implies in this instance that the torso twists as necessary to accommodate the tracing action.

33.11. In **33m** the design drawing is spelled out; the large size of the movement is not dictated here by arm directions but by a large amount of torso rotation and the general indication that the movement is spatially very large. A difference between **33l** and **33m** is that in **33m** the surface is not straight in front of the performer, but slightly towards the ceiling; this will make the gesture seem bigger, as if to suggest hills that are farther away.

For size of design, see section 8. Intermediate surfaces, see section 24.

33.12. Ex. **33n** is included here for comparison. Instead of design drawing, it uses deviations. In this example the directions are straightforward, but for

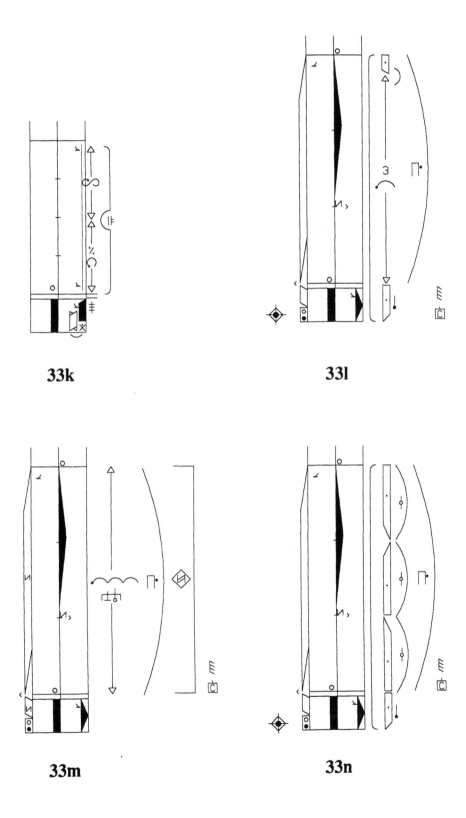

33k

33l

33m

33n

movement on an intermediate surface or using intermediate directions it would be difficult to write. In such instances design drawing serves the purpose.

33.13. Exs. **33o-r** show slight variations on an undulating pattern for the arms moving around the body. The arms describe half a circle clockwise around the body making small 'waves' up and down. In **33o-p**, the 'waves' are described by the arms as a whole. Ex. **33o** shows design paths for the arms. Ex. **33p** shows the same movement as deviations from the main direction of the arm movements.

33.14. In **33q** the 'waves' are described by the wrists (lower arms) and the movement is consequently more delicate than in the previous examples. In general, trace patterns of the wrist are made by articulating the elbow and/or shoulder joints depending on the shape of the design, the design surface and the placement of the limbs (cf. 6.2, 14.6). In contrast to **33o**, in **33q** elbow articulation is used to make the wrist rise and lower.
The 'passive' indication for the hands in this context means that the hands are reacting passively to the wrist (lower arm) displacement, in the sense of trailing behind. When the wrist rises the hand ends directed slightly downwards as a result. When the wrist lowers the hand ends pointing slightly upwards. The 'passive' indication does not mean that the hands are simply 'carried along' in the same direction as the forearms; this is standard performance and would require no additional indication.

33.15. Ex. **33r** is similar to **33q**. Isolated pin signs for the wrist mean minor displacements during which the wrist 'bulges' out of alignment with the other parts of the arm, implying a slight motion of the hand contrary in direction to that of the lower arm and performed as resulting from relaxation in the wrist joint rather than from positive wrist flexion.[24] This type of arm movement is seen in Bulgarian Ratchenitsa.

33.16. In all examples the movement begins in the upbeat. Exs. **33p** and **33r** have the advantage of clearly specifying that the small rise occurs on the upbeat and the lowering on the first count.

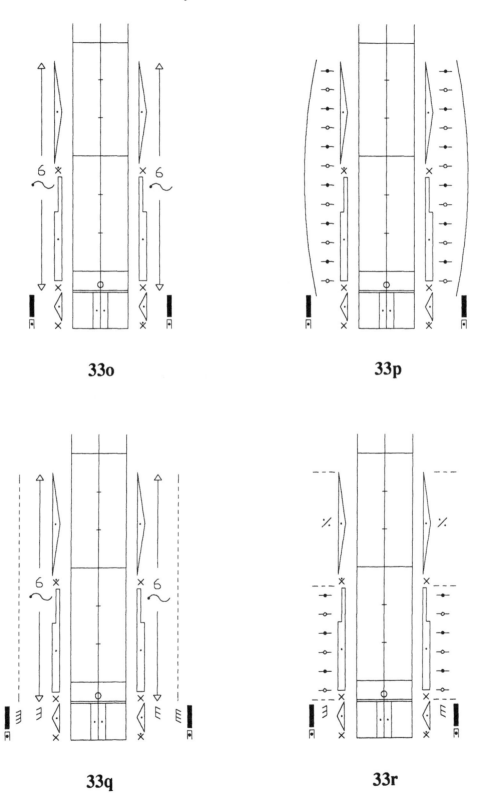

33o

33p

33q

33r

33.17. In **33s**, during the walking steps backward the arms perform a
contrary circular movement reminiscent of the engineering of steam trains.[25]
A pause is followed by a quick movement of the lower arms.

Because of the change of design surface from side to forward, surface
indications have been added to all designs for clarification. In the first design
body *surface* signs (for the back of the hands) and not wrist signs are used as
pre-signs, because the lower arms are not directed towards the design surface.
Cf. 14.7.

33.18. Ex. **33t** shows a scene from the *Green Table* in which the Profiteer
is gloating over an (imaginary) shining golden ring.[26] He first hides it behind his
back while he turns, then holds it before his eyes and does two steps. Then he
performs a hand gesture between each step to emphasize the precious object.

This gesture involves wrist flexion and lower arm rotation away from the
previous state of outward rotation and returning to it. These rotations must occur
so that the hand can trace the design on the stated side surface. Degree of
rotation is determined here by thumb edge facing. Cf. **33h**, end.

33.19. At the start of **33u** the hands draw in toward the shoulders before the
arms, passing through a circular movement, stretch out into the final pose.[27] The
transitory circular design is stated to be comparatively large and it is drawn as if
on the floor. It is necessary to state the surface of the design because with the
contraction in the elbow the surface is not obvious.

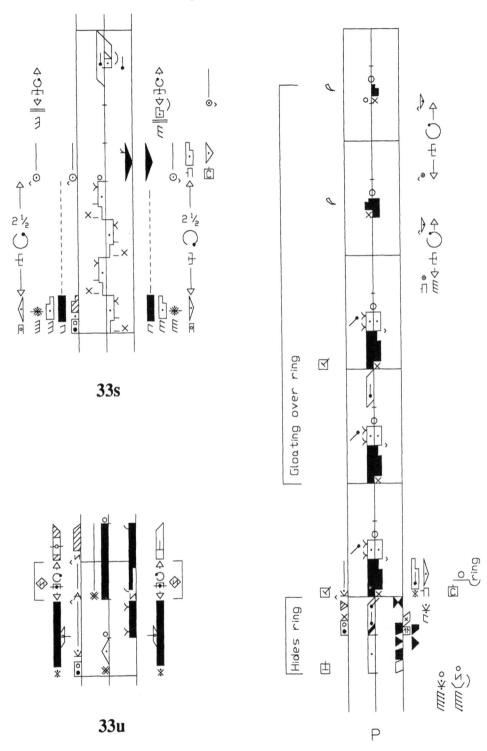

33s

33u

33t

34 Exact Timing[28]

34.1. Ex. **34a** shows exact timing of design drawing indications. 'Dancer's counts' are indicated in small print. The metre is 3/4. The small circles traced by the right foot are identical to those of the right hand. In the last movement the hand design blends with and is taken over by extension and rotation of the arm as a whole.

34.2. The movement can be counted in bars, i.e. in groups of 3 beats. The first introductory arm and leg gestures start in measure 24 and end 'on count 1' of measure 25. The first circles are completed 'on 2' (the beginning of measure 26). The second circles leading into the end position take all of the third measure and end 'on 4' (the beginning of measure 28). [29]

34.3. Exact lay-out depends on scale (the scale of this example is rather large). However, it is generally desirable to scale staff and symbols in such a way that the triangular end of the design path symbol plus a small section of its vertical line fall beyond the count line - within the first square if graph paper is used.

34.4. Ex. **34b** shows the tracing of a cross - as in the religious gesture. The design takes place in the general area in front of the body. Duration lines within the bracket show the exact timing for the first and the second movement. Note dotted line indication for the unemphasized transition from the vertical to the horizontal stroke. Similar movements and timing are used by conductors of orchestras. The alternating upward and downward strokes for a 2/4 metre, for instance, end 'on' the count.

For area sign, see section 9; for duration lines, see 4.5 (**4g-h**). See 10.3 for dotted line for transitional movement (**10g-h, 10j-k**).

34.5. Exact timing is used to show that the downward stroke of the designed cross ends 'on' count 1 (the duration line extends just across the bar line) and the horizontal stroke 'on' count 2.

Tick marks on the design drawing could be added to show subdivision of the design for timing (cf. **4f, 4g**), and a duration line could be added to show the timing of the small transitory movement indicated by the dotted connection line, but the notation seems clearer and more obvious without these additions.

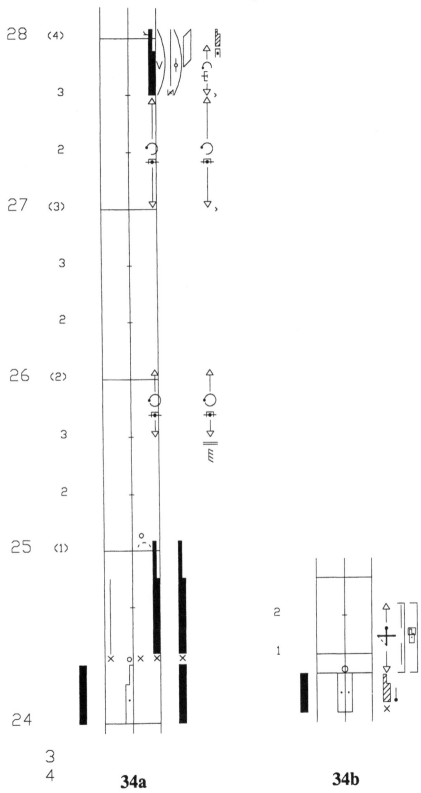

34a

34b

35 Trace Designs for Other Parts of the Body

35.1. Shoulder. In ex. **35a** the Miller's Wife in the *Three-Cornered Hat* by Massine is flirting with the Governor.[30] They are standing back to back and she is rubbing her shoulder against his, making him shiver in ecstasy. In the second measure however, she pushes him over into a step forward.

In the notation of the design, the dotted line as opposed to the continuous one (cf. 10.3) makes it clear that the repeated rubbing action is one of scooping down and up and that the accent is not on shrugging the shoulder upwards.

35.2. Chest. Through bending and stretching the knees and shifting the chest from one side to another, the front of the chest can describe a circular path, as shown in **35b**. In this example the design indication adds information not completely stated by the other indications.

35.3. Pelvis. A common design for the pelvic area is to describe a figure-eight design as if on the floor. This is achieved by a combined shifting and twisting action of the pelvis in relation to other parts of the body, and requires some degree of knee bend for smooth performance. Ex. **35c** shows this movement in its most basic form.

35.4. Ex. 35d shows a similar movement for the pelvis.[31] In order to indicate more detail the pelvis movement is analysed in terms of hip shift and pelvis rotation. The movement as a whole is quite small; the most prominent feature are the accentuated hip shifts. The action is paralleled in the movement of the arms.

For size of design, see section 8. For exact timing, see section 34.

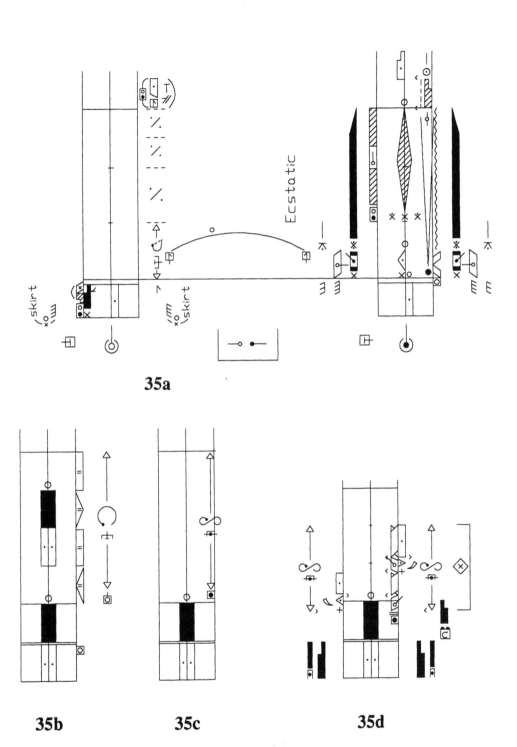

35a

35b   **35c**   **35d**

35.5. **Eyes.** Ex. **35e** shows the eye movement of someone watching a table-tennis match. If nothing else is stated, the movement of the eyeballs may or may not be accompanied by a slight head movement.

Note different possibilities of lay-out for the design. If two design path signs are used (**35e**) the design drawings are shown when they occur. If one design path is used (**35e'**) the design described is spread over the whole of the two-count measure.

35.6. **Center of weight** (center of gravity). Ex. **35f** shows design tracing written for the *center of weight*.[32] In contrast to design indications for the pelvis or the hips, design drawing for the center of weight does not imply any shifting of the lower torso out of alignment in relation to the rest of the body. Instead, the design is caused by displacement of the body as a whole. The determining factor is the location in space of the bulk of the body weight. Rising on the toes in standing causes the center of weight to rise, as would raising the arms overhead or pulling up from the arms while hanging by the hands.

In **35f** the design is caused by a combination of traveling sideways and rising and lowering through bending in the legs. While the actual circle described is elongated to the sides (an elliptical pattern) the stated circular design gives a clear idea of the desired movement intention. The movement performed by G is plain compared to the simultaneous, more stylized movement of L, N and R, who incorporate movement from the pelvis on every step and sway the torso to and fro in the opposite direction.

For design and whole body displacement, see also 22.4 (**22d** and **22g**).

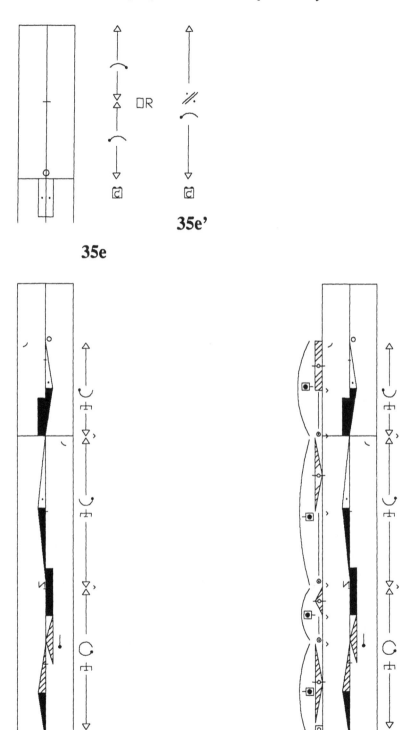

35e

35e'

G　　　　　　　　　　　　　　　　LNR

35f

36 Showing Shapes; Pantomime Gestures

36.1. Design drawing is particularly useful when the movement consists of showing a particular design or shape in order to convey a meaning attached to it. Symbolic gestures carrying a message are often hand or finger movements. Examples of static shapes (positions) are given in sections 28-32.

36.2. In **36a** the hands trace a figure-eight shape in front of the body.[33] This shape is clearly visible because the fingertips keep touching throughout and the whole of both hands show the path followed. The design is written for the little finger edges of the hands. These edges face the imaginary design surface throughout. Note the analogy with designs written for the palm of the hand (see 14.8, **14h**). The design is here emphasized by the hands changing their shape while moving through space.
  Movement indication for the left hand starts earlier than for the right; at first the right hand is merely adjusting to maintain contact at the fingertips.

36.3. Ex. **36b** is the well-known gesture meaning "He's touched in the head". The right index finger is close to the right temple. The design is written for the hand and not for the index finger or for the lower arm, because the articulation is to take place in the wrist.

36.4. Ex. **36c** is a pantomime sequence in which the performer is defining his territory, or indicating that he is standing in a box or an elevator. Design drawing is provided for clarification and quick reference. Although the timing for the design of each arm is divided in three sections, this is so obvious that it is not indicated by separate duration lines (see exs. **4g-h**). Gaps between direction signs already show the short pauses in the progression.

36.5. Ex. **36d** shows two performers walking towards each other and creating together the shape of an arch.
  For sign for 'shape', see sections 1, 28.

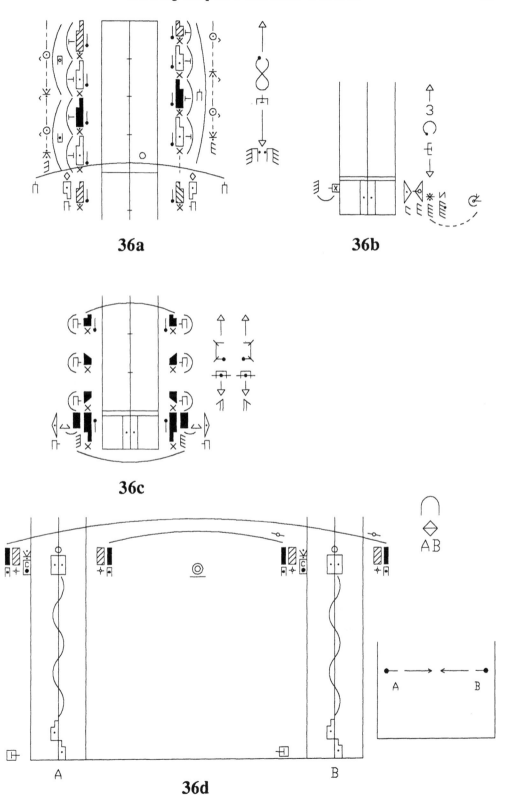

36a

36b

36c

36d

37 Design Drawing while Handling Props

37.1. When a design is traced while handling a prop, in some cases it is best to write the design for the prop itself and in others it is more practical to write it for the body part moving.

37.2. Ex. **37a** shows a Z-figure described by the right arm carrying a sword. Nothing is indicated for the sword. It may be considered self-evident that it is carried in alignment with the arm during the entire movement, and also that the sword is slightly lifted and carried to the left at the beginning so that the entire design 'fits' on the surface in front of the performer (for this last point, see section 15).

37.3. In Ex. **37b** a woman walks diagonally forward flicking her skirt with her left hand on each step.[34] It is possible, although usually unnecessary, to be more exact about the dynamics of this movement by providing a duration line for the design path to show where the accent occurs (here at the very beginning of the gesture) as in **37b'**.

37.4. Ex. **37c**.[35] This gesture with hat in hand is described in the usual way with direction symbols for the right arm. The resulting path through space of the hat is described separately as a reading aid.

37.5. Ex. **37d**.[36] The performer is waving a flag in his right hand. Although briefly interrupted, the design has a flowing quality throughout until the end of the sequence where the flag is pushed away from the body in a straight line diagonally up. The flag follows the movement of the arm; however, in this instance the separate statement of the design traced by the flag is particularly helpful to attract the reader's attention to the change of quality in the shape of the path at the end (from curved to straight).

The trace pattern for the right arm is related to room directions, i.e. independent of the two pivot turns for the body. The Constant Key is therefore used both for design path and directions for the right arm.

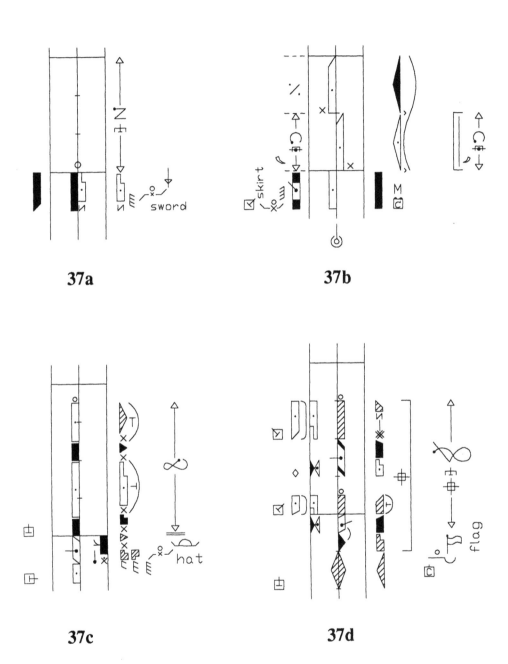

37a

37b

37c

37d

37.6. In the Chinese ribbon dance excerpt of **37e**, a ribbon is held in the right hand.[37] At the beginning the ribbon is folded so that all parts are held together; during the jump a flicking movement in the right wrist causes the ribbon to unfold. Both states of the ribbon are represented pictorially.

The arm is brought in front of the body (in the area of forward middle) from where a figure-eight pattern is performed towards the right then returning to forward, followed by a similar pattern towards the left returning again to forward. The designs are made by the lower arm with participation of the upper arm. Movement is continuous. Between figures and at the end the arm returns to the forward middle area.

Area sign, see section 9. Passive involvement of the arm, see section 7.

37.7. In example **37f** [38], because of lack of space the design path sign placed in the score is the abbreviation of the movement described in the box alongside the notation. Reference is made by an asterisk. The boxed indications have no time significance.

The ribbon is of light material and as the arm comes down it descends only gradually. Therefore the shape it adopts as a result of the quick zig-zag design of the arm remains visible when the hand is already down to repeat the movement.

Sign for 'shape', see sections 1, 28, also next example.

37.8. The whole turn of **37g** is performed holding a long ribbon in the right hand.[39] The effect of the movement described is that the ribbon forms the shape of a circle on the floor around the performer. In the column for the ribbon a dotted line indicates it is moving as a result of the action. The shape indication appears as the result of this movement.

The torso performs a countermovement enhancing the circular effect of the turn of the whole body.

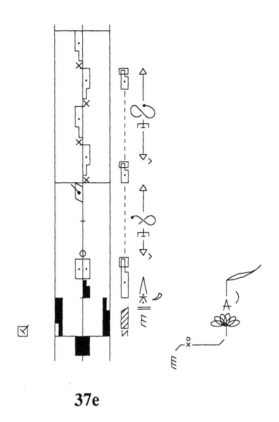

37e

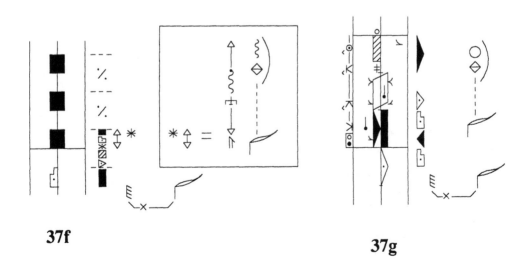

37f

37g

Notes

These annotations trace the major developments in "design drawing" and discussions on the subject.

They also discuss other relevant Labanotation rules and signs when different usages exist or issues are unresolved.

Finally, they identify the origin of reading examples from scores.

"ICKL 1979" refers to the *Proceedings* of the 1979 Conference of the International Council of Kinetography Laban. Proceedings of the 1989 Conference of the International Council of Kinetography Laban (ICKL) are not included.

In references to other sources, numbers refer to *example* numbers and not to page numbers, unless preceded by "p.".

Numbers in parentheses at the end of each note indicate where it relates to the text.

1. For references please refer to page 89.

2. This text is the first publication in book form on the subject. It is not presented in major textbooks such as Szentpál 1969-75, Hutchinson 1977 or Knust 1979 but has been in regular use in Labanotation scores.
The essentials (shape symbol, design path symbol, part tracing, size of design, situation of design, surface indication, etc.) were presented by Hutchinson Guest at the 1975 Conference of the International Council of Kinetography Laban (ICKL) and were largely accepted. An expanded version, much like the present text but with the exception of pins written in combination with design drawings (here sections 24-27) was presented at the 1979 ICKL Conference. Accepted were all items (ICKL 1979 Technical Report, I, 6) except "Size of the Design" (here section 8) which was passed at the 1981 Conf. (Tech. Rep. 8., p.27), "Situation of the Design" (see note 8), "Placement of Design for 'Ceiling' and 'Floor'" (see note 11) and "Determining Situation of Surface behind the Body" (see note 12). See also note 14.
There has been some discussion about terminology. At the ICKL 1977 Conf. 'Shape Writing' (the title of the original paper) was rejected in favour of 'Design Drawing' (Techn. Rep., 256).

3. The signs for 'accelerando' and 'ritardando' shown here, as well as the duration signs in 4l (4.9), are part of a more extensive set of 'time signs' including signs for a variety of concepts relating to time, such as 'as fast as possible', 'uneven pace', 'duration left free' etc. It is anticipated that most of these signs will be useful not only in Motif Description, where often timing is only vaguely implied in the relative vertical extension of symbols, but also in detailed notation, where each unit represents a defined (counted or measured) duration.

Time signs were discussed at ICKL from 1981 to 1985 (Tech. Rep. 1985 item

21) on the basis of the paper *Time Signs* by Hutchinson Guest and Szentpál. Further research was encouraged but no formal decision made. Time signs are occasionally used in Szentpál 1969-75. Not mentioned in Knust 1979 where, however, a different and smaller set of symbols is presented containing signs for 'accelerando', 'ritardando' and 'even speed' (764-66, cf. 763c-d). (4.8)

4. See note 3. (4.9)

5. Thus determining the body part sign to be used with a design path (i.e. naming the tracing part) is analogous with the use of joint signs with direction symbols. A directional change of the lower arm is written with the wrist sign, a directional change of the upper arm with the elbow sign, etc. In writing pre-signs before direction symbols, a recent tendancy is to replace the *wrist sign* by a *lower arm sign* to indicate a lower arm movement, etc. This is avoided here in conjunction with design path indications, as it is hard to say whether or not (or in which contexts) the image of the *wrist* tracing a circle in the air, for instance, suggests the same movement as the same circle traced by the *lower arm*.
    For the difference between wrist and lower arm (etc.) sign as pre-sign before *isolated pin signs*, see 33.14-15 and note 24. (6.1)

6. The precise implications of combining 'part leading' indications with design drawing have not been extensively explored. In each case the notator has to consider which description conveys the intended meaning in sufficient detail. For further examples, see **32c, 33l-n, 36a, 36c.** (7.8)

7. Knust 1979: 699a-d, Szentpál 1969-75: XV, 69a-d; both mention placement in addition bracket as in **8g**. The signs of **8e-f** (for 'as small/large as possible') are new. (8.1)

8. Situation of design dictated by preceding direction sign, deferred at the ICKL 1979 Conf. Accepted in 1981 for instances such as here exs. **9a, 9l-m**, ICKL 1981 Tech. Rep. 9, p.28. Paragraphs 9.1-5 were added for clarification. (9.2)

9. This set of symbols, combining a direction sign with the area sign, has been in use predominantly in Motif Description (Hutchinson 1983, p.61). The need for its application to detailed description grew out of notating African dances. Not in Knust 1979 and Szentpál 1969-75. It was discussed and deferred at ICKL 1981 (Tech. Rep. item 22). (9.7)

10. See note 13. (12.1)

11. This issue has been treated at some length because of calls for clarification (it was deferred by ICKL in 1977). The ICKL 1979 Tech. Rep. (11, p.28) accepts the way of writing of **16h** (**16j**, etc.), not mentioning **16i** (etc.). (16.1)

12. The original version of this rule was felt at the ICKL 1979 Conf. to need clarification (Tech. Rep., I, 6). It is now formulated in analogy with determination of directions for gestures (of the arms or other parts). (17.1)

13. There is a long history of ICKL discussion on the question of what is the best graphic symbol for 'a surface', 'a flat surface', 'a curved surface' etc. This comparatively unimportant matter has been deferred since 1975 and was still not settled in ICKL in 1987. The signs presented here are logical and serviceable. See ICKL 1987 Tech.Rep., 13, pp. 21-22. (19.5)

14. Sections 24-27 were not included in the original material agreed upon by ICKL in 1979 and subsequent conferences (cf. note 2). They introduce various devices through which to be more specific about designs and design surfaces, combining design drawing indications with other Labanotation symbols.

   Regarding the meaning of the isolated pin signs used in section 26-27, it should be noted that ICKL decided in 1979 that isolated pins indicate direction from the *proximal* rather than the *distal* center. However, reconsideration of this and similar decisions (cf. note 24) about pins taken in 1979 seems now called for. In our examples pins refer to the distal center. In Knust 1979 as in Szentpál 1969-75 the two principles are used alongside each other (e.g. Knust 1979: 151a and 331; Szentpál 1969-75: XV, reading exs. 20 and 21). This seems to be confirmed by general practice. Because the movement is always small, there is no danger of ambiguity. Note also that pins in deviation bows refer to distal centers. For pins referring to design drawings, it is obviously more convenient to relate to the distal center (i.e. the point in space where the design is being imagined) rather than to the proximal center of the tracing body part. (24.1)

15. The space measurement signs could be placed within the sign referring to spatial aspects (the 'diamond') as in **8a-f** without change of meaning; however, because they modify the *design* no ambiguity is possible and the diamonds can be omitted as a matter of abbreviation (cf. also **27e**). (27.1)

16. 'Back to normal' sign, not in Knust 1979 (cf. 789a-b), and not in Szentpál 1969-75. In both, the decrease sign fulfills both functions mentioned here. (31.3)

17. In **32a** the hold sign for 'retention in the body' for the wrist flexion indications is added for clarification. Some practitioners consider as an established rule that directional change for lower or whole arm does not affect wrist flexion and consequently they do not write hold signs in cases like **32a** (e.g. Knust 1979: 684g and cf. ICKL 1981 7, A 4). (32.1)

18. In this example divided columns indicate directions for upper and lower arms and the attached symbols directions for the hands. The hand directions are not accepted in all sources (cf. Knust 1979: 956). (32.2)

19. Reading examples taken from scores are in most cases slightly adapted either for simplification or to comply with more recent developments in the notation system.

20. From Leonide Massine, *The Three-Cornered Hat*, not. by Odette Blum in 1967 and completed by Jocelyne Asselbourg in 1973, copy Language of Dance Centre (LODC), London, copyright by Leonide Massine, ms. 409, the Governor

("Grape Duet"). (33.1)

21. From Leonide Massine, *Parade*, not. by Jocelyne Asselbourg in 1974, copyright 1974 by Leonide Massine, ms. 129-30 ("Chinaman"), p.7. (33.4)

22. From *The Three-Cornered Hat* (see note 20), Part I, section 1, ms. 50 ("Miller's Wife"). (33.5)

23. From Helen Tamiris, *Negro Spirituals*, not. by Lucy Venable in 1967, copyright Mr. W. Gibbons 1968, "Git on Board", ms. 9-11. (33.7)

24. Cf. Knust 1979, 151b. The 1979 ICKL Conf. agreed otherwise, namely that "a wrist sign followed by a pin will mean a movement of the lower arm, and "bulging" of the wrist will be written by one of the several other means existing in the system" (Tech. Rep. I, 3). However, it is not quite clear what these means are. Note also that a difference in meaning can be established by using the *lower arm* sign (as a pre-sign before isolated pin signs) for minor movements of the lower arm and the *wrist* sign (again as a pre-sign before isolated pin signs) for "bulging" of the wrist. This possibility seems to have been disregarded.
   The issue now seems to require reconsideration. Certainly in **33r** and similar cases the use of distal pins (as shown here) has been the predominant choice among notators both before and after 1979. Cf. note 14 about ICKL 1979 decisions on pins, and about the proximal vs. distal issue which has some bearing on it.
   For comparison note that, to all ends and purposes, the wrist sign means the same as the lower arm sign when used as a pre-sign before *direction symbols*. For *design path signs* a wrist sign, not a lower arm sign should be used. On this last point, cf. note 5. (33.14)

25. From James Cunningham, *Evelyn the Elevator*, not. by Lucy Venable and Mary Jane Warner in 1970, copyright by Mr. James Cunningham, rough partial manuscript, Dance Notation Bureau Extension at Ohio State University. (33.17)

26. From Kurt Jooss, *The Green Table*, not. as dir. by Odette Blum in 1980, copyright by Ms. Anna Markard and the Jooss Estate 1986, sc. 3 ("Battle"), ms. 94-97, the Profiteer (p. 119-20). (33.18)

27. From *The Green Table*, sc. 4 ("Refugees"), a Refugee Woman. Cf. *op.cit.* note 26, ms. 5. (33.19)

28. The conventional way of representing time in Labanotation is explained in section 4 and may be refered to as 'unit timing' as opposed to 'exact timing'. For a more thorough examination of the difference between exact timing and unit timing, see *Kneeling, Sitting, Lying* (forthcoming). See also note 29. (34.1)

29. Exact timing is only necessary in scores where a detailed representation of timing is called for. The conventional 'unit timing' version of **34a** (see also note 28) would be to write the first gesture in the space for the first count of bar 25 and the first circle in the space for the first count of bar 26, and to extend the

last gesture to fill all of the space for the first count of bar 28.

In comparison, the exact timing method shown in **34a** gives a better impression of relative length of movements and of the alternation between movements and pauses, especially when movement is relatively slow. (34.2)

30. From *The Three-Cornered Hat* (see note 20), ms.s 349-50 ("Grape Duet"). (35.1)

31. From Paul Taylor, *Aureole*, not. by Jane Marriett in 1976, copyright Paul Taylor 1977, 3rd. mov., p. 60, ms.8. (35.4)

32. From *The Green Table* (see note 26), sc. 4 ("Refugees"), ms. 19-20 (p. 138). (35.6)

33. This kind of gesture was used in the choreography of Doris Humphrey and Ruth Currier. (36.2)

34. From *The Three-Cornered Hat* (see note 20) I, 1, ms. 54 ("Miller's Wife"). (37.3)

35. From *The Green Table* (see note 26), sc.2 ("Farewells"), ms. 146 (p.71). (37.4)

36. From *The Green Table* (see note 26), sc. 2 ("Farewells"), ms. 75 (p.44). (37.5)

37. Not. by Chan Wong Shuk Chun, Louise, *From the Yue Di Dance to the Adventure on the Silk Road.* A perspective on the history and forms of Chinese dance with recordings in Labanotation, thesis, Faculty of Antioch, Part III, "Red Ribbon Dance", 1982, p. 317, mss. 3-4. (37.6)

38. From "Red Ribbon Dance" (see note 37), *ibid.*, ms.7. (37.7)

39. From "Red Ribbon Dance" (see note 37), *ibid.*, p. 318, ms.11. (37.8)

References

Hutchinson, A. (1977), *Labanotation*. The System of Analyzing and Recording Movement, Theatre Arts Books, New York (rev. 3rd ed.)

Hutchinson Guest, A. (1983), *Your Move. A New Approach to the Study of Movement and Dance*, Gordon & Breach, New York

Knust, A. (1950), *Handbuch der Kinetographie Laban*, unpublished manuscript (8 vol.) [written mainly between 1945 and 1950]

Knust, A. (1979), *A Dictionary of Kinetography Laban (Labanotation)* (2 vol.), MacDonald and Evans

Proceedings of the Biannual Conferences of the International Council of Kinetography Laban (ICKL), 1959-1987

Szentpál, M. Sz. (1969-75), *Táncjelírás. Laban-kinetográfia*, Budapest (3 vol., vol. I 2nd. ed., 1st 1964)

The Labanotator, bulletin, Language of Dance Centre, London, 1-, 1957-65 and 1979-.

Index

1.3, 5.2   etc.   refer to paragraph numbers
1e, 6a   etc.   refer to example numbers
*s*1, *s*2   etc.   refer to section numbers
*n*1, *n*2   etc.   refer to note numbers
p. 1, vii   etc.   refer to page numbers

cf. =   compare, see also

--   replaces the entry word

The more relevant references are sometimes given first, separated from the others by a semi-colon (;).
Dots following references indicate that not all occurrences are listed.

Lightning Source UK Ltd.
Milton Keynes UK
UKHW032032110821
388670UK00005B/165